T0330274

How to Stop Being Stuck with Your Academic Writing

To all of those special folks who glimpse themselves in these pages, and to the people who generously gave their time to be interviewed: your stories are my favourite thing. Thank you.

To Frank, who taught me how to play this crazy game.

To Caroline, who has spent her whole academic life waiting for my drafts.

And to my mum. Some people play their unborn children Mozart, but she chose the rhythm of stories being typed on an old, grey, Olivetti typewriter ...

How to Stop Being Stuck with Your Academic Writing

Seonaidh McDonald

Edward **Elgar**
PUBLISHING

Cheltenham, UK • Northampton, MA, USA

Published by
Edward Elgar Publishing Limited
The Lypiatts
15 Lansdown Road
Cheltenham
Glos GL50 2JA
UK

Edward Elgar Publishing, Inc.
William Pratt House
9 Dewey Court
Northampton
Massachusetts 01060
USA

A catalogue record for this book
is available from the British Library

Library of Congress Control Number: 2024934172

This book is available electronically in the **Elgar**online
Business subject collection
http://dx.doi.org/10.4337/9781789903966

MIX
Paper | Supporting
responsible forestry
FSC
www.fsc.org FSC® C013604

ISBN 978 1 78990 395 9 (cased)
ISBN 978 1 78990 396 6 (eBook)

Printed and bound by CPI Group (UK) Ltd, Croydon, CR0 4YY

Contents

Preface: Stuck

I am standing in the hall in the half dark. I have no idea what time it is; how long I've been standing here. The light from the study window strays through the open door. I can see the edge of my desk; the corner of a pile of paper. I stand there, waiting. Listening to my breath. I stand there, listening. Looking on now from a safe, 30 year distance I look still and quiet. But in my chest a war is raging. Fear battles promises. Confidence battles remorse. It feels relentless and unforgiving and exhausting. I stand there, frozen. I can't go in.

Slowly, I put my head against the cold door frame and close my eyes.

I am filled with fear and anger and shame.

The first time I got really, REALLY stuck was when I was writing my PhD thesis. It was a perfect storm. I had untenable personal situations at both work and home. I had wandered (wondered?) far beyond the realms of my discipline to places a long way away from where my supervisor could help me. I had designed a crazy thesis requiring mastery of half a dozen literatures and several research methods. I was exhausted and my confidence was shot. Everything that I could think of as happening in the future depended on the thesis being finished. Nothing else could happen until it was done. When I got stuck it was less like a thicket and more like quicksand. And because this had never happened to me before, I was really afraid. I thought that the writing had gone. Not that it was out of reach or had failed me temporarily. But gone. Forever. Taking with it my plans to be an academic, my idea of who I was and my sense of what I would do in the world.

Since you are reading these words you know how this story ends. I wrote my thesis, got jobs, wrote stuff, got more jobs, wrote more stuff and got a Chair. I have written lots of things. Some of them are quite good. But the fight that I fought with my thesis is still there. I still struggle to write. It takes me an inordinate amount of time and energy to start writing and keep writing and finish writing projects. Over the years I have learned a lot about being stuck and a lot about getting unstuck.

This is a book about writing and not writing. It is for everyone who struggles to write. It is for you if are new to being stuck, either because you are doing academic writing for the first time or because you have written prolifically for years but are unexpectedly stuck with a stubborn piece right now. It is for you if you are old friends with 'stuck' and want some companionship in the cul de sac you find yourself in today. It is for you if you want to stop being stuck. It is the story of all the ways in which I have been stuck and unstuck with writing and all the stories of all the people I have talked to about their writing. It is a memoir, a practical resource and a self-help guide. It is for you.

Acknowledgements

As I began to write this book, I realised how very grateful I am to so many people who have given me time, space and advice to improve my writing over the years. Some of you deliberately gave me advice, some have changed the course of my thinking completely by accident, some have been role models for me in aspects of your own practices and others have written by my side. Mentors, doctoral peers, colleagues, supervisors, co-authors, students, reviewers, teachers and editors, I have learned so much from you all. Thank you. I have done my best to pass it all on with great care to the next generations.

I need to say thank you to Francine O'Sullivan and her lovely team at Edward Elgar Publishing. Without her, I am not sure this would ever have been an actual book. It might just have remained a book in my mind's eye. Thank you for coming to my office to ask me for a book, for taking a chance on my idea and for never mentioning deadlines.

This list would not be complete without a mention of Neil Corall at Peacock Visual Arts whose antique letterpress the plates in this book were conjured upon. Thank you for encouraging my experiments.

Over the years that it has taken me to write this book, my family have seen a lot of the back of my head. They have never questioned the need to add 'writing a book' to the crazy list of things that actually need to be done in work and in life. They have never judged the inordinate length of time this whole thing has taken. And they have never complained about any of it. I can't tell you how much your love, acceptance and support mean to me. Thank you.

Introduction to *How to Stop Being Stuck with Your Academic Writing*

Writing, notwriting, notwritingatall and NOTwriting: some definitions

This is what writing looks like for me: writing is where I sit at my keyboard and type. I pause occasionally to look something up. I look out of the window a little, or get up to make myself a drink, but mostly I sit there peacefully and type. It can also look like printing out my manuscript and sitting down with a pen to read it and write comments on my drafts. Lovely. This is what writing looks like 100% of the time when I imagine it in my mind's eye. In practice, it actually looks like this about 15% of the time.

The rest of the time, it looks more like things I call notwriting, notwritingatall and NOTwriting.

Notwriting often also involves sitting at my keyboard. It is easy to spot, though, because my hands are not typing or writing. Often, I am looking at the screen, but, just as often, I am not looking at the words of the document I am notwriting. It is there, on the screen. It might be covered in other windows. I might even appear to be looking straight at it, but you can be sure I am looking through it. It can involve a whole panoply of splendid 'settling routines' (see Section 1, Sharpening pencils) or avoidance tactics (like email, especially email). But essentially it is a battle. Sometimes between me and the actual document (where to start, should this go in, have I said that, does this need more references …) but mostly, for me, it is between me and myself (Aaaaaarrrrrggghhh just *start*! You are wasting time, there isn't enough time, you haven't read enough, you are out of your depth this time, you cannot do this. Worse, you *can* do this, but you are NOT GOING TO). Etcetera. Notwriting is like sitting in front of one of those mirrors you get backstage in theatre dressing rooms with lightbulbs all around the frame so that you can see yourself clearly. Notwriting is like sitting in front of one of those mirrors staring at your own imperfections for hours. It is a soul-destroying experience which leaves us exhausted and undermined and stressed and guilty. I will do almost anything to avoid that mirror, so I have designed a work pace that hardly lets me sit down at it for a moment. I have arranged my life to be full of things which, much as I would LOVE to sit down and look in the mirror some more, mean I simply haven't got the time. Not today, anyway, or actually for most of the next week. After that, clearly I am going to sit right back down and get looking again (because writing is my priority), but not right now: I just can't today, sorry.

Notwriting is really hard. It is much harder than writing. It takes a great deal of energy and no small amount of ingenuity and denial. There are three paths out of notwriting: writing, notwritingatall and, my personal nemesis, NOTwriting.

If you keep up the notwriting for a long enough period, you may graduate into a semipermanent state of notwritingatall. This is where you are able to join up whole days of notwriting into long, wending chains stretching out over weeks and then months and even years. There may be a layer of dust involved, for dramatic effect. Desk drawers and/or boxes under your desk may also be required to ensure that when you are in the typing position, the thing(s) you are notwritingatall is(are) entirely obfuscated and cannot easily catch your eye. The modern, digital equivalent is files saved on an old laptop or written with outdated software that you are not even certain you could run on your work PC any longer.

On the face of it, notwritingatall is much less stressful. But unless you have actually, actively decided to let your writing intentions go for good, they will continue to mutter in the background of your workspace like the low machine hum of an air-conditioning unit that needs a service. On and on. Only just audible, and almost entirely edited out by your brain, but there in the background. The sort of noise that you would notice with great relief if it were to suddenly stop. There are only two known cures for notwritingatall: the first is to make a firm and final decision to let that project go, acknowledge that it will never be done, recycle all your notes and drafts and delete the files. And breathe as your mind feels the relief of not holding on to it any longer. The second cure is to dig it all out and move it consciously back into the notwriting pile. Let it go or get it done are the only remedies. Anything else is a holding pattern.

Then there is NOTwriting. NOTwriting is when you keep your notwriting up for ages, but instead of it getting smaller and quieter and dimming into notwritingatall over time, the notwriting sort of stacks up on top of itself and gets much bigger and angrier as time goes on. Its voice gets louder and more insistent until it is shouting inside your head and it is hard to hear anything else, or remember where you put your keys or eat a whole slice of toast without wandering off to do three other things in the middle. Eventually, you stop being able to hear the words and just experience it as a sense of urgency and doom. For me, at times in my life, this has spilled over into clinical depression and various other delightful things like anxiety, colossal impatience, even more colossal sarcasm and shouting at people trying to do their jobs. Unlike not-writingatall, which can be generally not doing any of several writing projects, NOTwriting tends to be a face-off with a very specific, single writing task (like the relationship with my PhD thesis[1] that began this book). If this is where you are standing right now, please get support. If you don't know where to start, try your doctor. No book on writing is going to be enough to sort this lot out. **You need to get yourself well first**, then get some support for yourself and your writing practices to get yourself back to normal, low levels of everyday notwriting where other people and some of the stuff in this book can help you.

In a way, NOTwriting is better than notwritingatall. At least you are doing battle with the damn thing. It is in the front of your mind. I don't recommend standing there long though. It is not good for your physical, mental or emotional health. At all. If you can use the stress and distress this causes to alert yourself to what you are doing, the NOTwriting can give us the impetus to make a shift to another phase. Don't just stand there with your hands over your ears trying to turn up the volume on your denial to cover the shouting in the hope that if you do that for long enough it will get bored of shouting and dwindle away into notwritingatall. Step out. This is just a phase. It is not THE END. The writing is still there (not here, right now, but it is still there: it hasn't gone altogether). There are other phases that you can try, if you are willing. Here is my NOTwriting action plan:

1. Get well. Intervene in your own health. You don't need to be 100% fit and healthy in mind, body and spirit to write, but you clearly need to be better than you are right now. An academic writing career is a marathon, not a sprint. This is not hell for leather, downhill to the finish line and then it will all be over. *This* writing might be over, but the next writing will be standing there, expectantly holding its hand out for the baton. This could go on for years! You need to slow down your running speed so that you can keep going. Personally, I like to walk. Both in my marathon analogy and in my real life. Walking shifts my thoughts and my body at the same time. Mother nature's great BOGOF.[2] And sleep. Try more sleep.

2. Get support. That might look like your doctor. It might look like a counsellor. It might look like a mentor or a writing buddy. It might look like your cat if she is very patient like mine and listens to all manner of nonsense about how and why I am stuck.

3. Get unstuck. The bulk of the rest of this book is about things I have tried that have helped me get unstuck, as well as the favourite habits and mindsets of lots of other people I have interviewed about their writing practices. Try some of these and see what happens. Take a step back and try to see this not as a big pile of DOOM but as a puzzle that you can solve. I realise that when I say 'take a step back' this is easy to type and can be

VERY hard to do. That's why you need to do 1 and 2 first. Because it is way easier to do when you are feeling well and when you have someone else's perspective of yourself and your writing to add to the mix.

To begin with, I thought that these might be phases. You know, so that you had to work through one to get to the next level, like you would on a computer game. Although at one point it looked like they only worked backwards. Writing gave way to notwriting which gave way to NOTwriting. But I have learned that this is neither inevitable nor irreversible. Over time I have noticed that the phases are not mutually exclusive. Right now, I am: writing this book; notwriting a couple of papers with two different co-authors; and I have been NOTwriting a paper with one poor co-author for so long now that I am verging into notwritingatall on that project. I can also be writing a section of something and notwriting another bit of the very same thing. Did I mention that I was VERY skilled at notwriting? Here's what I have found, though: despite it feeling as though all kinds of things can hurry the fall between writing and notwriting, there are lots of things (not one big, shiny cure-all, but lots of tiny, varied and ordinary things) that can also pave the path from notwriting to writing. I have put them all in here to save you time searching for them yourself.

A NOTE FOR THE SCIENTISTS

The majority of my academic writing experience is in writing with and for social scientists. One of the things I was keen to do when I was interviewing other academic writers about their writing for this book was to find folks from a wide range of disciplines. The scientists I spoke with were not immune from being stuck, but they did see a separation between the research process and the writing process that for social scientists and humanities folks (especially qualitative scholars) is very blurred indeed. I first noticed this blurring when I asked a bunch of entrepreneurship scholars to describe their qualitative writing practices and got back a load of data on their data analysis processes (Smith, McElwee, McDonald & Dodd, 2013). Writing and analysis are not always so distinct for the social scientist as they are for their scientific counterparts. As a result, some of what is discussed here may stray (in a scientist's view) outside the remit of what they understand as writing into processes of sensemaking they would be more comfortable with labelling design or analysis. For scientists, my patient interviewees explained, the act of writing is not as integral to the research as I had assumed and is really mainly 'reporting results'. They definitely recognised the 'stuck' thing, though, and some of them felt that this was a familiar part of the earlier stage of research design and experiment formulation, where the figuring out happens. That helped me to see how we may be complexifying the writing processes in social science by conflating 'figuring out' and 'writing' and sometimes also 'analysis'. Because if something is really difficult, why wouldn't you multiply it by something else just as difficult? It also made me realise that for some of the scientists reading this book, the terms, practices and processes may seem a wee bit alien at times. Bear with me: I mean well!

HOW TO USE THIS BOOK

The trouble with most texts on writing is that most of them privilege one technique and suggest that you (a) practise it a lot and then (b) stick to it forever. I know that over the years I have tried most of the practical suggestions set out here. Lots of them have worked for a time and none of them have worked forever, either because, although they are effective, they are not easy to maintain for me personally or because they lend themselves to sabotage by other aspects of work or life. What has always worked, though, is changing tack: trying something else or layering the tasks up in a new way.

The other issue with some of the self-help texts is that they deal with the mechanics of the problem. They are keen on practical suggestions. In my experience, writing is not just a fight with habits and systems, or even words. It can be all those things, of course, but essentially writing is a fight with yourself. In this book I will offer many practical tips and systems for writing, but I will also offer new ways of looking at the problem and suggest ways to deal with the personal and emotional elements of (not) writing.

Begin with the section on Writing, notwriting, notwritingatall and NOTwriting (p. xii). This contains the definitions that will help you make sense of the rest of the book.

Then you need to have a look at one of the first three sections. These are presented in a linear way, but in real life, they are in a chain of interconnectedness. I use the following diagram to help me think about how they relate to each other.

HOW THIS BOOK IS ORGANISED

The three main sections of the book are set out in the way in which they are most helpful for most people. They are also in order of how easy they are for most folks to do. I've done it in this way so that I can help you make a difference to (how stuck you are with) your academic writing as quickly and effectively as possible.

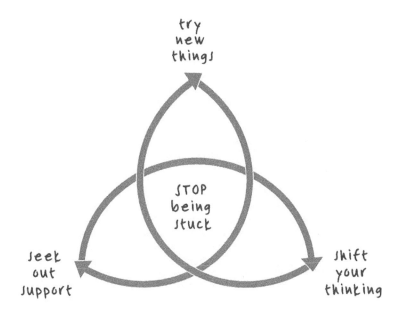

Section 1: Try New Things

This section contains a great big list of stuff you can try. They won't all be 'new' new things because you'll have heard lots of them already and maybe tried some before we met. I'm certainly not going to claim I invented them. The idea is that if you are stuck, then it is a good idea to do something other than what you are doing right now. That kind of 'new'. One or two of them verge on belonging to Section 2, in that they involve other people, but on the whole these are all things that you could try on your own.

If you are notwriting, then I recommend this as an excellent place in the book to start. It contains a load of ideas about things you can try to get yourself (or someone you are trying to help) unstuck. You will notice that they are all different and some of my suggestions even seem a bit at odds with others on the very next page. The idea is not to do all of them, or try to follow every suggestion at the same time (although I have used all of them over the years). Read through some and if you find something that resonates, then stop reading and try it out. See if it works for you. This section is intended as a source book of things to play with in your writing practice, rather than an edict on how to mend your ways. Bear in mind that you might need to try a few of these before you find something that works. Don't worry: just keep trying. Also remember that even if something is a miracle cure on Tuesday, by Thursday afternoon it might have lost its charm. Don't Panic.[3] Just have a look for something else to try. Keep changing tack. Keep not panicking. Keep trying new things.

If you try loads of these and either they don't work for you or their effects fade and die very quickly, then you might need to try some ways that someone else can help you. Have a look at Section 2.

Section 2: Seek Out Support

If you have tried some things in Section 1 and are only having very limited or short-lived success with getting unstuck then it might be time to consider getting help from another human being. Read through Section 2 and see what your options could be. Not all of these include finding a kindly and wise academic mentor (I realise that these are not always thick on the ground, or immediately available), some of them are about peer support and light-touch accountability methods for which any old academic peer or kind person will do. Sometimes these support mechanisms work on their own, sometimes they have a kind of cumulative effect when layered up with some of the Section 1 stuff. Also: when I am really stuck, I need more than one kind of (and person for) support, so don't stop at one if there are more things you could try.

If you have given some things in both Section 1 and Section 2 a good try and you still feel stuck, or constantly on the verge of stuck, then it could be that you need to have a think about how you are thinking about your writing. Try Section 3.

Section 3: Shift Your Thinking

If you suspect that **you are notwritingatall** or **NOTwriting** or you have tried a dozen different things from Section 1 and/or Section 2 and you are still in fact stuck, then you might want to look at Section 3. This section deals with the third route to getting unstuck: changing your mindset. The root of the problem might be something that needs a change in your thinking about yourself or your (not)writing or a different understanding of the stuck. I realise that having the section on thinking after the section on doing is going to seem a bit odd for some people. But it is because it is the doing that is often the fastest way to get unstuck. Rather than let this book become a distraction in its own right (I see you), I'd like you to try some things long before you've read the whole book. Putting the sections with all the things to try in it first is my way of trying to trick you into doing that.

Once you have read the definitions, you can choose from the following ways to find a starting place within each section:

1. Read through the section and make a short list of three to five things that appeal to you. Take those one at a time (or in combination, if that works) and try them out in your next writing session. If they work, keep going; if they kind of work, adjust them a bit and pair them up with something else; if they don't work at all, just try something else.
2. Flick through the section and pull out a suggestion that randomly catches your eye. Give it a go and see what happens, as per 1.
3. Some of the sections suggest other 'kindred' sections and you can follow those trails through the book. You'll notice that many of the trails in Section 3 lead back to suggestions in Section 1. That's not a coincidence. It is because thinking probably isn't going to be enough to get you writing again on its own: you will need to do some things too.
4. If you feel like you are definitely stuck but need to have a think about what kind of stuck you might be, then have a look at the Where should I start? Flowcharts (pp. 123–129) which will guide you through a series of questions and give you suggestions on useful starting points. There are flowcharts to guide you to ideas about how to tackle confidence challenges, time challenges, non-writing challenges and writing skills challenges. Working through the questions in each flowchart will match you with a starting place in the book. If your challenge is with a specific, recalcitrant writing project, there's a flowchart for that. If you are ready to stop being stuck, check out the 'OK, let's do it!' flowchart for some direction on places to start if you haven't got the time or inclination to flick through the whole book.
5. Alternatively, you could let the universe intervene! Open the book at a random page and read the section you find there. Try that and see what happens.
6. If all else fails, sit down somewhere nice with a lovely drink, start on page 1 and read it like a book.

Section 4: Improving Your Writing

Once you get writing (you will get writing!), there is even a section on improving your writing. But if that just piqued your interest and your thoughts went to 'Ah ha, I can skip all this and just find out how to do it properly/better', then might I gently suggest that you read this section LAST and only once you have got yourself thoroughly unstuck.

Section 5: Institutional Problems (and What You Might Do about Them)

If you are trying to understand how to inspire a whole group of folk to write, then take a look at the section on how institutional problems can set up barriers to people writing. These have been separated out because they are much harder to shift and almost impossible for a single person to change in the short term. It is possible to shift them, but it will need a concerted effort, led by management, to really make things change because often these are deep-seated cultural norms. I've made some suggestions here of things to aim for and how you might allocate any limited resources at your disposal. I have also included a short piece on how to work out whether a specific department or faculty is going to be supportive of your academic writing for folks looking for new jobs.

Section 6: Resources

In the final section, you will find a bunch of stuff that might be useful in your quest to get yourself or your colleagues unstuck with academic writing.

NOTES

1.   See Glossary entry on Thesis.
2.   This stands for Buy One Get One Free, an offer beloved of supermarkets in the United Kingdom.
3.   You were right, Douglas Adams (1979), you were always, always right.

1 try new things

2 seek out support

3 shift your thinking

1. Try new things

In this section there is a whole circus full of suggestions which are all possible paths to getting unstuck. They are a mixture of things to play with in your writing practice and ways of getting different kinds of support. Every one is slightly different. Every one has got somebody unstuck. You can pick more than one and layer them up in infinite combinations. Not all of them will be for you and not all of them will play nicely together. In fact, some of them are pretty much the opposite of each other! There is no need to work through them systematically or even to try them all. Just give some a go and keep trying things until you get unstuck. You could just flick through until your eye lands on something you find interesting or unexpected. You could follow the trails of suggestions at the end of some of the paragraphs to find related ideas. Or you could read through them all and go back and try your favourite. If the list seems a bit overwhelming then you could look at Where should I start? Flowcharts (pp. 123–129) to help you find a starting place. The only rule is this: Try Something.

If you try some of these and they make no difference at all, you might either need someone to help you (see Section 2) or you might need to think through some of your thinking first (see Section 3). If the thing you tried stops working, just shrug and try something else.

BLANK PIECES OF PAPER

There is nothing worse than a blank piece of paper. Unless it is a thesis (or book!)-sized blank piece of paper, or more terrifying still (close your eyes) a completely blank file. The cursor waiting. Blinking. Tapping its fingers. Rolling its eyes. I tend to overcome that first blank page by writing notes. I write incoherent (and if they are handwritten, also mainly illegible) jottings that cover some space and whose main purpose is to stop the blankness of said page.

If you really can't start, try a title page where you can put in your name and contact details. If you still can't start, go for a walk, tidy something up, make an appointment with the dentist, hang out the washing or delete 10 emails. Just do something that gives you a sense of progress for a few minutes. You'll be surprised how micro confidence boosts can affect your writing. Note to self: don't do *all* of these, otherwise it will be the end of another day and the page will still be blank. If it gets towards the end of the time you have set aside for writing and you still haven't begun, set a timer for 10 minutes, take a deep breath and write any old thing till the buzzer goes. Then stop and feel the gladness and relief of starting. Let it flow through you and remember that you CAN do this. Now, you can type or write normally for a short time or pack it in safe in the knowledge that the blankness (paper or writer, you know best where the blankness really lies) has been banished and that the next time writing will start just fine.

SHARPENING PENCILS

When I was allegedly writing up my PhD thesis and living in a tenement flat in Stirling, my mum called one afternoon to see how I was. 'I'm fine.' I said, 'I'm washing the stairs.' I am a second-generation academic. There was a careful pause at the other end of the phone before she asked, 'What should you be doing?'. Here is a prime example of when doing the settling things we all ritualise at the start of our writing, such as getting a cuppa and putting on the PC, turn into avoidance without us really acknowledging it. Difficult, protracted and unpopular tasks are the best choices for displacement activities because they put off the moment when you have to start typing for ages, give you a sense of progress, of being a good citizen and deflect any negative judgement you have of yourself for not writing with positive judgement of yourself for having achieved the displacement task. It's an accomplished sleight of hand. You need to catch yourself in this trick and call it out if you are to stop it. For me, this was made easier by the fact that my mother was never fooled by my errant/exemplary behaviour.

My mum began writing (and putting off writing) before the advent of PCs and so in our family this kind of displacement activity is known as sharpening pencils. I am a genius at this. I have got it down to such a fine art that I can fool myself for weeks by super-league (should that be fantasy-league?) pencil sharpening. I have learned to use work as work avoidance. Oh yes. I take on projects with the specific (subconscious) aim of undermining my writing plans by genuinely being too busy to write. The more afraid I am to write, the bigger the job I find. On coming back from my first maternity leave with my confidence at rock bottom I actually wrestled a whole research methods module off a colleague. I taught every postgrad in the faculty that year. I could not have found a more comprehensive and exhausting way to use my days and shut out every possibility of writing if I had tried. In my younger years, not really being sure how to press on with my writing independently of my great mentor, I asked my boss if I could do an MEd part time. To give him his due, he tried to stop me. He tried his level best to give me sound advice about my writing career, but I was determined. This is just washing the stairs but scaled up into mammoth writing displacement activities that can be measured in written off (pun very much intended) years rather than lost afternoons. In fact, it is only in writing this just now that I have actually seen them for what they are: ways of doing a good job that gain approval in one realm of academic life and also stop others from having high expectations of my academic writing: sharpening pencils.

DRAFTS

If you are a perfectionist, or the horror of supervisors, reviewers or even co-authors reading what you have written is holding you back, then you need to find a way to convince yourself that what you are writing is just a draft. Nobody will see it but you. Make it safe to start writing.

There are lots of ways that you can do this. Over the years I have known folks who used all sorts of formatting tricks to lull themselves into an 'it's just a draft' state of mind. One colleague used coloured paper (she favoured yellow) to print out stuff that was for her eyes only. A more subtle approach is to use grey or unbleached paper for drafts. If you share a printer with every colleague on your floor then this is a very time-consuming and logistically difficult approach, but if you have one to yourself, you could even fill one paper tray with draft-coloured paper and the other with white. In the days when printers printed on only one side I kept a stock of partly used paper in my office and printed drafts on the blank side. I inadvertently got myself caught in an Escher[1] staircase situation late one night by printing out a draft of a paper on the other side of a much earlier draft (but starting on a different page) and then started editing it as if it were double sided. After half an hour of editing myself round in some elaborate circles and a few minutes of blind panic when I thought I had somehow lost the new draft, I realised my mistake and now give the first printed side a wee check before I begin, to save any further heart-stopping moments or endless mazes of editing. At home, where my printing is still pretty low tech, I am still working through the backs of draft thesis chapters by students who graduated many years ago. Reduce, reuse, recycle!

If you are one of the many people who enjoy formatting as a pencil-sharpening activity, then changing margin sizes or fonts can also give a feeling of 'draft' to the piece you are working on and reduce the starting inertia. Almost all of the journals I publish in stipulate boring, common or old-fashioned fonts, so when I am writing drafts, I like to choose something a bit more uplifting. Don't go mad or you won't be able to read it quickly, but do use something that you find pleasing.

Almost all of the journals I publish in stipulate **boring**, common or old fashioned fonts so when I am writing drafts, I like to choose something a bit more **uplifting.** Don't go mad or you won't be able to read it quickly, but do use something that you find pleasing.

That way you create the idea that nobody will ever need to read what you write, and if you have anxiety about your writing being good enough or fear the judgement of others is stopping you from starting, then this can be a useful way to get going. See also Drafts in this section.

STARTING AT THE BEGINNING

One of the fastest ways for me to get stuck is to try to start at the beginning. Several of my interviewees shared the technique of just starting somewhere. Some start with their favourite part, some in a random place, some with whatever started the idea for the paper: a data-driven paper would start with a results section; a piece driven by a model that's being applied or tested would start on the theoretical framework; and a paper which is dedicated to setting out counter arguments or agreements between disparate literatures would start with the literature review. Me? I just start anywhere. I use the headings technique described here (see Placeholders in this section) to brainstorm a bunch of chunks of text I know I am going to need and then I write under whichever heading catches my eye (this is how I am typing this book right now!). Sometimes I finish a whole section, sometimes the cat intervenes, but if I get stuck or uninspired, I just type somewhere else. If I am very tired indeed, I have been known to sort out references for a while just to keep it going sans inspiration.

STOPPING IN THE MIDDLE

There is a lot of advice for writers along the lines of not stopping at the end of a paragraph, or even a sentence, but in the middle so that your next beginning (in time) is easy because it is finishing a sentence or paragraph that has already been started (in words) (see e.g. Wolcott, 2008). This may have its roots in Hemingway's description of his writing: 'I always worked until I had something done and I always stopped when I knew what was going to happen next. That way I could be sure of going on the next day' (Hemingway, 1964). So, when you do get writing, you could try leaving yourself a wee note about what you were thinking of doing next (Dear Seonaidh, you have two more points to put in here: one about leeks; and the other about triangles. Love, Seonaidh) or stopping in the middle of a paragraph. Or even in the middle of a …

GOALS

When we are writing, we tend to focus on a range of goals that are pretty unsuitable: submit the thesis; finish the paper; give your co-author a draft. These are rubbish goals. First, they are waaaaayyyyyyyyyy too big. Second, they are singular; mono goals if you will. And third, they are output focused. Let's take these one at a time.

Goals That Are Too Big

If you are reasonably far through your project, skimming along, writing every day and putting in a few hours, you might reach one of your goals in a couple of weeks (draft), a couple of months (paper) or a couple of years (thesis). All of these goals are so very big that life will need to happen in between your writing. Eating and sleeping and other work and other people and doing your tax return and going to the supermarket and doing your recycling and … My point is that the writing goal you have chosen depends on all the things between the times when we are sat down writing. And that is far too may things to try to figure into the equation. By the same token,[2] every time we sit down to write, we can guarantee that we won't hit our goal. How is that helping?

Plus, if I told you that I was going to try to learn to play a tune on a musical instrument that was strange to me, what would your advice be? Amongst all the lovely things you might suggest as helpful, I bet you would tell me to practise. There are two things here that respond well to practice: writing and celebrating. To practise writing, have a look at the sections on handwriting, or drafts. There are folks who suggest starting with writing prompts or free writing (see Boice, 1990 for descriptions of how to use spontaneous writing, for example) to get you started, but you can just as easily brainstorm one that's relevant to the work in hand. As for celebrating, if you are currently notwriting then I'd like to bet that you are either not used to celebrating wins in your writing or that it is something you haven't done for a while. So, let me suggest that you practise. One of the side effects of having a big, far-off goal is that you don't get much practice with the celebrating (see also Section 3, Celebration). Now I know that there is a part of us that sometimes feels like notwriting = bad person and writing = good person, and that only good people should be allowed to celebrate. This withholding of joy (see also Doing joyful things now in this section) does not in fact drive us onwards towards writing. We think it might, but even if it works in the short term, on the whole it just makes us joyless and out of practice with the celebrating. As well as notwriting. (Way to make notwriting the focus of our entire existence!) Celebrating helps, so why plan to do less of it? Why not practise it all the time so that we get really good at it?

Make smaller goals. Like, much smaller. Smaller than that! Seriously, take the goal you had in mind after I said, 'smaller than that' and halve it! You have to make a goal that is appropriate to the amount of time you have to write. That way, you can achieve your goal every time you sit down to write. And celebrate that every time you achieve your goal. If you only have a two hour gap between meetings to write, give yourself a goal that you can achieve in 90 minutes. Not a two hour goal that means you have to run the length of the building, skid to a stop at your desk and pound out words in a sweat before repeating the performance in reverse to get to your next meeting (the next meeting is always in the next building but one and you never notice that until two minutes before it starts because you have been focused on writing, writing, writing and not on whatever requires your presence elsewhere afterwards). This might work for a day, but you (and all your colleagues in the meetings you run into ill prepared and out of breath) will very soon get sick of it, and then it will just be another failed strategy to beat yourself with. Allow yourself time to move between tasks gently and quietly, and also to have a drink and use the facilities.

When you are starting out with this, though, you need your goals to be tiny. Tiny and short term. So, rather than 'edit the paper', you need to aim for 'edit one page'. Instead of 'finish chapter 7', I want to see you plan to 'finish a paragraph on eels'. In place of 'format the references', I'd like you to try 'format five references'. Then celebrate each one. These micro goals are a really important way back from notwriting to writing. As my writing starts to flow again I do make my goals a bit bigger, and I am always, without fail, tempted back to a list of 'finish the paper' goals as my confidence and rhythm return. But it is always a mistake. A true triumph of hope over experience – and I always have to reinforce my tiny goals again if I want to stay out of notwriting.

Also: big goals mean fewer celebrations means less chocolate (see Rewards in this section) less often. Choose more success with added smiling and extra chocolate. Do your own maths, people.

I am going to give the last word on tiny goals to another dear friend. Once, on leaving her office where we had been discussing a huge potential writing project, I flippantly remarked that Rome wasn't built in a day. She looked over her glasses at me and said, 'Yes. But parts of it were, Seonaidh. Parts of it definitely were.'

Singular Goals

One of the things I used to do as a researcher and as a supervisor when I started was to try to guard against any situation that would mean having multiple writing projects. When writing got hard, I would start to say no to all the things in the vain hope that if I was strict enough with myself I would get the most important thing done, and then I could start some new and exciting things. But I took this too far, let it spill into my actual life (remember academic writing isn't the same as life) and stopped myself doing anything at all apart from the important thing that wasn't getting done, in the hope that this would help get it done. Spoiler alert: it didn't help me, in life or with the writing. At all.

Now, a certain amount of this kind of thinning out our 'to do' lists as if they were carrots is healthy. It lets the carrots that are left grow to full size. And I have been known to not say no to an awful lot of things. As writing gets hard and my confidence wanes, the fact that folks are asking me to do things makes me feel useful and wanted and cheers me up, and I often mistake that cheery feeling, which is the relief of finding that I am not entirely useless, with a positive feeling towards the things I am being asked to do. And because elephants (and writing projects) in the distance seem small and manageable when they are in fact just far away, and much more interesting than whatever I am banging my head on currently, I say yes. Then my 'to do' list can get a bit out of hand. You can see how this might lead to overwhelm and loss of confidence, and soon a vicious cycle is firmly spiralling downward to NOTwriting. So there always comes a point when I have to go back and say no (and oh, it is so much harder to take back a yes six months later than just to say no in the first place, but I am a ridiculous optimist) and shorten my list. But that's not what I am talking about here. What I mean by a singular goal is when you get your edited list and prioritise it. You tell yourself that you will do this writing project first. You will not distract yourself with any other projects until this one is completely done. I used to do an equivalent thing with my students, making them focus on one chapter until we had a whole draft before releasing them into the next part of the thesis. It took me years to stop doing this to myself and to stop giving this advice to everyone else. Funnily enough, when I was interviewing prolific writers for this book, I found that they all had multiple writing projects on the go. They were writing a book, co-authoring a thing with their post-doc, shaping up an idea for a paper (maybe it would be a special issue) with the woman in the next office, had nearly finished a book chapter with an old friend and had another three papers in various stages of readiness with a long standing co-author in another part of the world. The most prolific authors were working with different colleagues across several distinct lines of research (or even across disciplines). The reason that multiple projects worked so well for them was that when they got stuck (and they ALL got stuck), they simply had a cuppa and a stretch and changed projects. In other words, the most productive strategies involved working on more then one thing at once. This works best for me when I have things at different writing stages. One in a storyboard or outline, one in a pile of things that I need to read, one in a half-eaten draft (aka bits of things and loads of headings, some with random paragraphs), one in draft, one or two on the desk of a co-author, one needing a polish, one waiting for references and formatting, one submitted. Progress on any one of these is progress. But crucially, progress might look different for each one because each task is different. If I am going on a train or to a meeting where public transport means I will arrive a couple of hours early, I will choose the editing task. If I am really tired, I will search for references. If I need cheering up, I love to format things for my target journal or make bonny diagrams. Forward is forward. Allowing multiple projects seemed to me from the outside looking in like a messy, inefficient, overwhelming business. From the inside, I experience it as bringing an element of freedom of choice, as creative and productive. Damned if the 'separate' projects don't start informing and inspiring each other, too. They won't stay in their boxes, offering each other new references, novel ideas for structure and, most of all, they always seem to egg each other on. I've become a big fan of multiple goals.

If this sounds like chaos to you, or the definition of stressful, then maybe, like me, you were being too literal in your idea of what writing multiple things would look and feel like: I had an image of some kind of frantic, plate-spinning trick where you were trying to keep everything going at the same time. But in fact, it looks more like a zoom lens. I will foreground one thing on any given day, focusing on that and letting all the others fall away, unfocused, into the background. But if I get stuck, I know I can take a breath and refocus on something else rather than just keep staring at the thing I can't do. The trick is to have lots of things that you *could* focus on, but being able to put aside all but one of them to focus on at any moment.

Output-Focused Goals

I have left the best one for last. The worst thing about having something like 'finish a paper' as your goal isn't just that it is enormous, it is that it is output focused. This means that however much you do, you won't reach your goal today. Not even if you complete a full draft and give it to your co-author to read. Not even if you submit it to the journal. Not even if you send off your second round of revisions. Not even the day, some time in the future (the distant future if you are a social scientist), that you sign copyright forms and send back the proofs to the publisher. The only day that you can say it is 'finished' is the day it finally appears in print. This may be anything from weeks to months after you have actually done any work on the paper. So it is quite far removed from your experience of doing any writing and also out of your control. Imagine training a dog like that. You observe puppy doing a charming trick. A random number of months later you make a fuss of puppy to congratulate him on his trick and add a wee treat. Good boy! I'm sure your doggy will be thrilled, but it will not reinforce the trick-doing behaviour because it won't occur to him that the trick is what the reward is for. In short, output-focused academic goals are not linked in time or agency to your writing behaviour. You are going to have to find yourself a better training routine for this particular trick.

So, once you have cut your big, far-off goals into tiny little slices of eminently achievable right-now writingness (see above), there is an even bigger trick you can pull. You can change the currency of your goal altogether. By changing the currency I am referring to changing the units that we use to measure our progress. The analogy here alludes to recalculating the value of, for example, Canadian dollars in Icelandic króna, but in truth we are swapping our obsession with monitoring our writing outputs (measured in words, pages or chapters, for example) into considering how much time we spend writing (measured in minutes and hours). This seems like an intellectual trick, but bear with me: more words, pages and chapters can represent progress, but cutting words, pages and chapters can also represent progress. More importantly, when we are notwriting, perfectionism is sometimes at the root of the problem (see Section 3, Perfectionism). Perfect words are the enemy of anyone trying to get unstuck, and writing and rewriting the same thing until it is shiny only to delete it the next day is a routine that fuels notwriting. I need you to let go of how many words you are writing AND how good or bad they are right now and just learn how to open a channel of flow so that you can have something to edit some day in the future. To do that we are going to focus not on your output but on the time you spend writing.

This was the thing that eventually got me back from NOTwriting to writing. When I was wildly and madly stuck with my thesis I got to the stage where I couldn't actually go into the room it was in. I used to stand on the threshold of the door and try to will myself to go in and sit down at my desk. There were days when I didn't manage. In fact, there were days when I ran past the doorway in a desperate dash for the land of notwritingatall, but mostly I sat in my flat, feeling the presence of my unwritten chapters but not being able to look at them or even go into the room they were in. Sometimes I would go in and sit down and hours would pass with me staring blankly at the screen. Eventually, a friend who was not easily fooled by my 'fine' rebuttal to all enquiries as to the state of the thesis (she was writing her own thesis, but that is another story) realised that I had completely ground to a halt and made it ENORMOUS in my head. She turned the whole thing round with a single sheet of paper. At this point in the (not)proceedings, I had written rough drafts of seven out of eight chapters. They all needed stuff doing to them and I needed to write my conclusion. She sat me down and patiently asked about the specific things each chapter needed. She wrote out a list of all the things left to do in every chapter. And then she changed the currency. She took each item on the list and asked how long it would take me to do each one. I quoted a number of hours. She doubled them. Partly on the basis that I was not exactly full of health and vitality, so she reasoned that my progress would be slow to start with, and partly because she realised I had no idea how much time it actually took me to write in a sustainable way. We had been undergraduates together and she knew well that I could write 5000 words in a day-and-night binge, but also that writing a thesis was way beyond the help of an all-nighter. A thesis, like an academic career, is a marathon, not a sprint. Sprinting will only slow you down in the long term. As I had never really learned to write 'normally', my idea of what could be done was at best based on the binges of my binge and bust-writing patterns and at worst pure fantasy. So, once she had tempered my idea of how long each thing would take with a reality check, she drew a series of wee boxes. One for every 15 minutes. She taped the sheet of paper, full of empty boxes, to my study door. She gave me a coloured pen and told me that I had to go into the room with the thesis, sit down and do something, anything, to progress it for 15 minutes and then I could colour in a box and leave the room. I got to colour a box in if I spent 15 minutes raking for a reference, 15 minutes reading an article, 15 minutes writing a sentence, 15 minutes writing a single heading. It didn't matter what I did, as long as I spent 15 minutes in the room working on the thesis, I could colour in a box and leave. She had changed the currency from 'complete thesis' or even 'complete chapter' to 'just do 15 minutes'.

I thought she was mad. I thought it wouldn't work. I stood outside the door of my study after she had left and I looked at the boxes. No judgement. No quality checks. Just time. I mean, this could never work because I could just go in there and format a table for 15 minutes. Or move a paragraph from one chapter to another. Or look for that reference for that paper my supervisor had given me an unpublished copy of. Or make a pile of these papers that I need to put into the reference list for chapter 4. I'll just put them all here. That one is for chapter 3 … and before I had realised I had gone in and started starting. 15 minutes passed and I coloured in a box and stepped over the threshold. I looked at the list. I looked at the clear space on my desk. I went through to the kitchen and looked out of the window. I came back into the corridor and looked at the box I'd coloured in. She had only given me four boxes for day 1. I went to get a cup of tea, set the timer on the cooker and went back in. I felt giddy with achievement and cried all the way through the next 15 minutes of writing. I completed my four boxes, went straight to bed and slept for 14 hours. I was triumphant and I was as exhausted as if I had worked for 15 hours, instead of four blocks of 15 minutes. After about a week I made the boxes into

30 minutes, and then eventually 45. After a while I didn't need the wee boxes anymore. She made me promise not to do more than four hours a day so that I wouldn't trigger the binge writing I was so reliant on because that only led to the kind of exhaustion that ended in notwriting.

Colouring in the handwritten boxes was my first experience of celebrating my writing goals. This scheme was perfect for me in that moment. My friend made my goals teeny tiny, allowed me to practise achieving and then celebrating them and she changed the currency from output to time. By using a combination of two of these powerful goal-shredding techniques, she unlocked the path for me to walk back from NOTwriting to writing. Of all the writing strategies I have tried, the combination of making goals tiny and changing the currency of the goal to time is the most powerful for me when I find myself notwriting.

The bad news is that (for me) this wasn't a one-time fix. I have needed to learn these lessons over and over. Every time I get stuck in notwriting I experience the panic of believing that I cannot (not now) and will not (not ever) write again. Over the years, the experience of being stuck and getting unstuck has changed this into a panic that I cannot write today. Often, by the time I have allowed writing tasks to come to the top of my list (see Writing first in this section) I have not left myself any time to be stuck at all, only time to write downhill, with a clear run and the wind behind me. Only leaving what would be nearly enough time in the most optimistic of circumstances is a path straight to stuck for me. Most of us experience this as a ramping up of pressure, which makes beginning difficult and enjoying our writing impossible. By contrast, I have noticed that wide open days full of unstructured time and blank pieces of paper have a similarly disabling effect on my writing, but that is a different story. The pressure of having to write this, and only this, right now, and keep writing until I am 'finished the paper/draft/grant application/chapter' catapults me back to the situation where I can only have a singular, large goal. I regularly use the third trick of 'changing the currency' to break into this cycle of panic, notwriting, panic, more notwriting, PANIC …

After I had been doing this for many years I found, like most of the lessons that I have learned the hard way, that this was already a thing. It is known as the Pomodoro technique, after the tomato-shaped kitchen timer of the Italian chap who coined this term (Cirillo, 2018). I discovered that making tiny, time-shaped goals was already really popular in management efficiency circles. My mum used a version of this to mark student work in the 1970s (a task we both hate with a passion) and counselled me to mark for 40 minutes and take 20 minutes off every hour. Pomodoro is basically a planned balance of time working (in our case, writing) and time not working, ruled by a timer. You can choose any combination of time writing and not writing, but when I am stuck I find that the traditional 25 minutes writing, 5 minutes not writing (and I mean not writing here, no notwriting in your downtime allowed!) both too long and too short. Try taking the writing timer down to 10 or 15 minutes to start with and balance it with an equal amount of downtime until you build up your practice a bit. Buy yourself a tomato-shaped timer if it pleases you, but I find some mechanical timers a bit clicky and distracting (is it just me who starts to find that countdown clicking a bit sinister and unnerving after a while? On bad days I can hear the clicks as a judgement, so now you know what it is like inside my head!) so I use a digital one on my PC. On good days I don't set a timer for my downtime, but on days when I am very tired and distracted, I time that too, otherwise I do the very un-Pomodoro technique of 25 minutes writing and then two days of phaffing about until I realise that my PC is still on and, turning off my screen saver, find to my genuine surprise and horror that I was supposed to be writing. So, if you think you might wander off or even 'forget' to sit back down after your five minute break then go ahead and time yourself. Or set yourself a number of short stints per day, as my friend did, bearing in mind that your upper limit should be four hours in a day (see Writing for four hours each day in this section), unless the circumstances are genuinely urgent. That's not 'make my co-author roll her eyes' urgent but actual 'I will lose my job' urgent. There's a distinction there that we all lose sight of from time to time as the notwriting gets bigger and bigger in our heads.

One more thing: do not use your timed downtime to do other forms of work. Or housework. No emailing someone, making a quick phonecall, doing your grocery shopping online or cleaning the bin. These all qualify as five minute tasks, but they do not, repeat, do not, qualify as downtime. Downtime looks like: dancing in the kitchen; going outside; staring out of the window; listening to music; walking and stretching; smiling at your cat/colleagues/children/self; getting a glass of water; closing your eyes. Academics can be very bad at doing this downtime thing in the first place, and really quick to deny ourselves any as soon as we have a deadline. See Breaks in this section.

DOING JOYFUL THINGS NOW

A lot of the time my logic goes like this:

I am notwriting today. Therefore, I am a bad scholar. Therefore, I must not allow myself to do nice things. [frowns at lack of writing] Repeat until end of available writing time.

Abstinence from the joyful things in life does not make you write better or faster or more voluminously. It just makes you write less joyfully. And, if I'm honest, on the whole: less. We get into a kind of lack of delivery, self-punishment, lack of delivery, self-punishment cycle that makes us feel smaller and smaller and less and less confident, and guess what? Our writing gets less and less and smaller and smaller too. Now I know that rewarding yourself when you are notwriting can feel counter intuitive (or counter the whole-premise-of-our-upbringing/schooling/cultural norms for some folks). But we are not going for 'compliant author' here; we are shooting for 'inspired author', so quit frowning at yourself and try a new recipe:

I am notwriting today. Therefore, I am uninspired. Therefore, I must find a way to inspire myself. [dances in kitchen] Writes a wee bit before the end of available writing time.

Disclaimer: you don't have to actually dance in the kitchen. But you do need to find something that works for you. Something joyful. Mine look like: Smile at the cat. Marvel at a tree. Speak to a friend. Walk a bit. Cook something lovely. And best of all: put my feet in the sea. What are yours?

It is great to use joyful things as a reward (see Rewards in this section) but you don't need to save them all until the writing has finished. If you are feeling flat and dull, you can use them to help you find a lighter place to write from. If you are serious about writing consistently, over a long period of time, you need to get less serious about it. You had better also take a look at Creativity (this section) because you are going to need to build joy in systematically to be able to keep yourself in that space.

WRITING FIRST

It is a truism in the management world that the urgent will always get done before the important. What this means for your academic writing is that although you genuinely believe it to be important, it often falls off the end of your working day because your time is hijacked by something that is urgent. You may plan to write but then when you look at your email you find your inbox full of requests to stop what you are doing right now and answer a question that is urgent for somebody else. It is amazing how often and how automatically we adopt other folks' urgent as our own. Pause for just a second and set that request into the context of your own daily priorities (or even your own values and beliefs about what is important in this corner of the world we call academia: remember there are lots of good ways to be a great academic, and you get to choose yours). Is it urgent? Like *right now* urgent? Or only *today* urgent? Or even *this week* urgent?

Actually, I have discovered that very little in academia is genuinely, life threateningly, business closingly urgent. Really, unless the Border Agency[3] turns up looking to determine whether your reporting systems are adequate, nothing that you do today will impact on the health or welfare of any student or member of staff if you let an hour or even two go by before you get it done. Of course, we think lots of things are urgent and we treat lots of things as if they are urgent. If you, like me, stray into 'virtuous avoidance' very easily then you will allow all the 'urgent' things to kidnap you because they allow you to skip your 'important' list. We do this because (a) often the urgent things are easier and quicker to do and (b) someone notices if we do them (and if you don't write today, probably nobody will). These characteristics give us an immediate sense of progress, agency and self-esteem that chipping away on a much larger, longer-term, more important goal does not (if you are nodding at this last point, see Goals in this section).

Plus, we kid ourselves that because these requests are 'urgent' they are a one off. It is because of this upcoming accreditation. Once that is past ... It is because Christine is off ill. Once she is back ... It is because we have a recruitment freeze. Once that is lifted ... And my favourite: it is because the exam boards are next week. Once they are over ... Every day we let urgent things slide up our priority list because we tell ourselves that they are unique, but when we look back over the last few cycles of our academic lives we realise that many of these things (a) happen regularly (exam boards), (b) are predictable (if you set your sights on an accreditation, that will cause everyone loads of extra work) or (c) are university policy (running with no slack in the system means that one major illness, parental leave or delay in recruitment in your team means the system will break unless everyone overworks).

So what if we begin the day, before we even open our email, before we even switch on our PCs (yes, that means before we see all the things that other people think are urgent – don't be too hard on them, they haven't yet realised that nobody will die and they are probably just rushing from one thing someone else deems urgent to another without pause for thought themselves), by deciding what is important? If you are blinking wildly at me right now it is because you have no idea what is important and what would happen if the urgent emails stopped (hint: they won't ever stop). It has never happened and so you have never planned for that and your important is something so vague and far off that you don't actually have a clear idea of how to begin doing it right now. Fair enough. Time to get a plan. Have a look at Goals in this section. In the meantime, let me give you a clue: it probably involves academic writing.

Ask yourself this: if you could go forward five years in time and ask your future self what the most important thing you could work on today would be, what would s/he say? Better answer that student who can't find the thing you have clearly explained on your website. Quick: reformat your marking rubric in line with the university's new policy. I'm guessing not. All these things need to be done, of course. I am not suggesting you don't do them. I'm suggesting you don't do them *first*. I'm suggesting you don't do them in the order they hit your email inbox. I might even (steel yourself) suggest you don't do them today. So, what should you do? Your future self would probably tell you to do something in line with either your values or your priorities.

When I am asked why I became an academic I always quote Terry Pratchett, who reckons that most folk become priests because it is 'inside work with no heavy lifting' (Pratchett, 1993, p. 26). Or I tell people I was not ready to leave school. But secretly I love reading and writing and new ideas and I wanted to use those things to make a difference in the world. My academic field is sustainability and I have a passion to understand why people do (and don't do) the things they do so that I can offer that understanding back to the world in the hope that it will help people help people to change their lives in what I see as positive ways. Most of us end up here not just because the world doesn't quite know what to do with clever people and think it would be a good idea to put them all in the same building together (newsflash: this is not always that good an idea), but because we want to push back the forefront of knowledge in some small but particular way. So, one of the ways your future self might answer your question about what is important would be to redirect you to the difference you want to make in the world that brought you here in the first place.

If the idea of navigating importance with your personal values and passions is anathema to you, then let's look instead at the more practical game we are all engaged in: career progression. In five years' time, what job do you want to have? Which accolades will you need to pass into that place? Do you need a single author article in a 4* journal?[4] Start with that. Do you need to bring in three quadrillion pounds in research funding? Maybe start writing a grant proposal. If you are currently sitting on bits of a doctoral thesis, I think we all know the answer to this question! If you are not sure what you need to progress then ask people. Show your CV to someone kind at the level you want to get to, or someone lovely who has managed people making that transition, and ask them what is missing. The key words in that sentence were 'kind' and 'lovely', just in case you missed them. Ask a few people and then decide what your important is. Some will undoubtedly answer out of their own fears, biases or agendas, but some will be able to look past themselves and offer advice that is genuinely in your best interest. Identifying an important milestone towards your own 'next step' is a good way to align your important with your priorities.

Right, that's enough whimsy: it's time to get radical. Once you have decided what your version of important looks like, and you have carefully crafted some goals, you need to start putting your writing first. If it's important, let's treat it accordingly. More important than email? Yes! So do it before you open your email. If you are a morning person, give that part of your day to writing. I was first given the advice of writing before I did anything else by a colleague, who not only wrote before he opened his email, but didn't open his email until he was about to break for lunch. He was from an older generation of scholars who got all their summonses and directives in meetings or by memos in the post and had developed a routine when he was a young PhD student of breaking off from his writing to stretch his legs by walking to the staff common room to look in his pigeonhole just before lunch. His view was that just because our communications had become instant, they were not really any more urgent than they had been in the 1960s and so checking twice a day, before lunch and late afternoon, would still be plenty of checking to do in a day. I have another (really prolific) friend that wrote before breakfast. That is a step too far for me in all kinds of ways.

I am not a morning person. If I am brutally honest, my best time of day is the wee small hours of darkness when everyone else in the house is sleeping. And that is all fine if your writing is going well and you don't have any other responsibilities apart from your writing. If your writing is not going well, then spending half the night staring at a screen whilst cursing inwardly is not the healthiest position to be in. Most of the activities that you might do to distract yourself from your notwriting and the people you would call on to talk about it are probably not as available at 3am as they might be at 3pm.

You could try getting yourself a writing buddy in a different time zone. I used to work with a colleague in New Zealand and we would tag team our way through drafts, each blasting out a couple of hours at the start or end of our day and then pinging them back across the ether to greet the other on waking. Synchronous meetings to actually plan and discuss our writing were trickier to schedule, but the writing itself was quite quick. I did love that feeling that someone else was writing while I was sleeping, but it probably wouldn't have worked if we hadn't already known each other quite well in the first place.

Writing in the night worked fine for me right up until I became a person who gave 9am lectures. I persevered, though, making myself both mentally and physically fragile, until I had kids. 3am became less attractive and, for a while, because I couldn't do 3am, I didn't write. I began to work in the evenings, staying at work after everyone had gone, because 6.30pm on a Friday evening in your office has a very similar feel to 3am in your house. The lights go out and you can take your shoes off and only the security staff will know. It wasn't a long-term solution, though, as I just got exhausted and lost all my resilience again. I was horrified to realise that I was going to have to start writing like a grown up: in my office at work during my work day. In the end I managed to block my teaching so that I could write in my study at home during my work day. So my version of 'writing first' looks quite different than my colleague who writes before breakfast, but it comes to the same thing. We have both looked at our work weeks, thought about the kind of time that works best for our writing and then stolen it for ourselves, working everything else around it. I have a friend who 'blocks' her semesters: all her teaching is crammed into semester 1 when she runs around teaching all the things, ending with a marking marathon and a very quiet winter break. She does this so that she can spend semester 2 running around her local parks and green spaces every morning before spending the day on writing projects and minimising time in the office.

There was no consensus in my data about when the best time of day is to write, but there was definitely a consensus that there was a best time of day for everyone. When I heard people talking about writing first thing in the morning, I used to feel my heart sink. I knew I could never do that and so felt like it wasn't worth trying. But you need to look closer at what your best time of day is for writing and see how to make that work for you. You can all breathe a sigh of relief, night owls. It does not have to involve being coherent and articulate at 6am if that is not what will serve you right now (or in my case, ever!). And bear in mind that what works for you in this stage of your life might not be useful or achievable forever.

WRITING RETREATS (AKA CIVILISED BINGE WRITING)

Sometimes the best thing to do is pack up your laptop and take your stalled writing project on a wee holiday. A writing retreat is where you suspend all the other things in life in order to just write. The easiest way to do this is to go away. It doesn't have to be far. But it works best if you are away. A writing retreat is a very useful kind of 'away'. You can do this on your own, with friends or colleagues or join a retreat run by someone else. Search online and you'll find there are almost endless options. Some of the best ones are quite structured, allowing writing and non-writing time and sometimes offering communal activities or social events in the downtimes, if being on your own for several days feels a bit alien.

The writing retreat is the acceptable, planned version of a writing binge. If, despite trying to incorporate writing into your other routines and responsibilities, you find that you still yearn for long writing episodes, or you revel in this kind of focus and immersion, maybe you just need to submit to the idea that you are a binge writer and plan happy binges. Ones where you don't have to hurl yourself headlong against a career-threatening deadline and risk your physical and mental health to get things done. Ones where you check out of your life deliberately for a set amount of time and then work limitlessly but joyfully on your writing.

Be mindful that many of us fetichise this kind of time but are not actually productive when we get to it. Also note that several of the authors who write about academic writing are very scathing of writing binges (Boice, 1990; Silvia, 2018, for example), and this approach is presented as negatively as the wishful binge writers present it positively. It definitely works for some people, though (Evans & Smith, 2023). So, you know, if it seems like it would be the answer to some of your stuck, I would recommend trying it once or twice to see whether it actually works for you. Stop using your energy to mourn the unsuitability of your job, boss, children, seven donkeys (real or metaphorical), lack of funds and caring responsibilities and focus instead on finding an ingenious way to make this happen for yourself: team teach; do someone else's marking so they'll teach your third years for a week next semester; house sit for someone; bribe a family member; pay for a school trip; inquire about respite services; volunteer for a work trip that would also give you some unstructured time; go to a conference and, instead of attending the least worst session, attend only those presentations that you genuinely want to see and write in the rest. Brainstorm with a trusted colleague about how you could make this happen for each other.

I have a tiny retreat every time I am stuck in a hotel room for work: room service, laptop, no distractions. Bliss. You don't even need to stay overnight. You could take yourself off to the public library in the next town for the day. What you do need to do is 'retreat' from everything else. As a minimum, you need to switch off your work emails. Tash Aw says, 'I find that a writer's retreat involves, quite simply, turning off my devices and checking my emails only once a day, or sometimes not at all' (Gunesekera & Kennedy, 2015, p. 89).

A friend of mine who is a single mum has a kind of reverse writing retreat where her parents come to stay with her for a couple of weeks and take care of everything. I mean everything: school run, meals, pets, appointments, shopping and all the after-school clubs and social engagements. Then she puts an out-of-office message on her email to say she is away and does not have access to her email. This leaves her free to roll out of bed in the morning, deal with her own breakfast and write. She writes all day. She goes out for walks, she meets friends in cafés to write some more. Sometimes she writes late into the night or gets up crazy early and writes for a while and naps all afternoon. She doesn't leave home, but she does have freedom from every obligation that would normally take emotional labour to process and break up her day.

A word of warning, though: if you take annual leave to do your academic writing because it is the only way to have permission to have a break from all the other kinds of work, don't let that be the only leave you take. A retreat can be a glorious, productive experience, but it is still work and it does not qualify as a holiday. Take an actual holiday as well.

If you try allowing binges and either you don't find them helpful for your productivity when you give yourself time and permission to binge or you can only manage to binge write in the desperate circumstances an imminent deadline creates, then I need you to acknowledge that you are not a binge writer. You are someone who only writes under intense pressure and you need to think about why that is (see Section 3 for all of the clues to follow), and consider taking a step away from the damage it may be causing you and/or the innocent bystanders in your life in binge and the barren wasteland of exhaustion it may be causing post-binge. This was my story.

DITCHING THINGS

This skill is really important to me because it is the opposite of my own super-power, which is gathering up all of the things. Things that people would like me to do; things that I don't have enough room to fit in the paper I am writing today; things that seem interesting (and crucially, different from the thing I should be doing right now). All this makes for a crazy 'to write' list. It has taken me many, many years to understand that not every idea that would make a great paper needs to become a paper, and even those that do, do not all need to be written by me.

I was mentored by a senior colleague who was gifted at this. In lieu of an annual review, every year she would sit down with me, make me show her my 'to write' list and see what she could wrestle off me. 'This paper,' she would declare, 'has not moved forward for years: I don't think it will ever happen now.' And she would take it off my list. 'This co-author,' she would say, raising an eyebrow, 'has let you down so many times before: it is time to stop writing with them.' Pencil line through two papers. 'These data,' pointing at another optimistic entry, 'are out of date now: you need to let this go.' Her challenges were shocking to me, whose only method of taking something off the list was getting them completely finished. I had only mastered the art of putting things on. I was making my list longer and longer, heavier and heavier and more and more impossible to deal with. She was always on my side and I always fought back, against myself.

Sometimes her insights would send a shard of clarity shining across my list and I would suddenly see that the paper was doomed, or dull, or too late or just too time consumingly difficult to have any merit and I would happily strike them off. She was giving me permission to not torture myself and I was grateful. Other projects had become so ingrained in my list that it was really hard for me to shift them – even when I saw that she was right. These were usually projects bound up with data that I felt obligated to do justice to. Qualitative data are especially hard to leave in a cupboard. When you have deliberately gathered up lots of voices, opinions and perspectives, not writing them up feels like you are ignoring, undermining or betraying them in some way. Other papers represent promises you have made to fellow academics and some of those are really hard to go back on, even if time, distance and progress have intervened. Yet others are hard to let go of because of all the time I feel I have already invested in getting them to whatever sorry state they are currently in. So I developed a (secret) middle ground: archiving. Shhhhh don't tell her!

I have put this section in here, rather than in Section 2, because, although I need help to do it, there is no real reason why we couldn't do this for our own 'to write' list. At least in theory. If you know your list is longer than your career span already, give it a try, and if you turn out to be as rubbish at it as I am, pick it up and drag it over to Section 2, Get a writing mentor to see whether they can help make your list more realistic.

ARCHIVING THINGS

You know when you are clearing out your wardrobe and you find a piece of clothing that you cannot be certain that you will never wear again, that might not even fit, but that you still love and cannot part with? The declutterer's advice is to put it in a box, store it for six months or a year and if you haven't thought about it or needed it in that time, you can get rid of it. Some recommend that you don't even open the box. You probably don't remember what was in it and you definitely don't need it. I do a version of this with my 'to write' list. When my mentor drew attention to papers that were languishing on my list, taking up headspace and never getting done but I couldn't bring myself to let them go, I archived them. I have a folder on my PC for every paper. I made a new folder called 'Shelved' and I moved the folders of the papers I was probably not going to write into it. Then I took the paper off my 'to write' list. The paper was all still there, could be revived at any time if I needed it and I avoided the pain of having to delete drafts or data. But the whole thing rolled out of my sight, off my conscience and, as far as my mentor was concerned, it had gone. Relief! All those papers that I was notwriting (or even notwritingatall) just became things I wasn't going to write. All the power of my mentor's ditching without the bravery and decisiveness of having to actually delete things. A 'soft' delete, if you like.

Side note: whilst I was writing this, it occurred to me that I had never once reinstated a paper from my Shelved folder to my 'to write' list.

GIVING PAPERS AWAY

Another version of ditching that I have occasionally practised is giving papers away. Writing projects that are at the stage of a glorious data set, a bunch of articles identified and a splendid idea where you have written a conference paper or first draft make excellent candidates for this. Ask yourself: who would love this? Or even: who would benefit from this? Gather up your half-eaten paper and go and see that person and ask whether they would like to take the lead on it. Make sure they understand that you are not going to do any more actual work on it and that you want your name in the least prominent position in the author list (for some disciplines this is last, for some it is second last). In exchange for your data, draft and ideas, they will write it up as a paper and never speak of it to you again until the day it is ready to submit. When it is ready to go you should check it over because, you know, your name is on it and you need to make sure there are no crazy statements or hateful comments or other hostages to fortune, but resist the urge to meddle with it or slow down its passage. The paper is saved and your list is shortened: win, win! People who love to write but hate to gather data, or people who are in a hurry to write big papers but don't have time to get their own data, are often thrilled by this kind of deal. Win, win, win! If you try to give it to another person with an equally ill-fated 'to write' list you will of course get short shrift. Or if you ask someone who is as slow a writer as me, all it will get is slower. But if you genuinely believe that the stuff has merit and that if you don't do something with it then it will just haunt and torture you, then give it a try. People are always a bit surprised by me trying to hand over my papers. I have had a few fights over me insisting my name is last, and some of the papers never got written, but that's OK because it is no longer me notwriting them! I have had some success with this strategy over the years and have never regretted it.

ABSTRACTS, TITLES AND FIRST LINES

I have a friend who spends a day or two at the outset of every paper (even a conference paper) crafting the perfect abstract. She gets started by setting out exactly where she is going and in doing so she reaches forward in time to the finished paper, drafting and editing her abstract until she can see the whole paper clearly in her mind's eye. Only then does she write the paper to serve that abstract. One of my interviewees does a similar thing with the introduction of the paper.

I know folks who start with the title of the paper. They audition different titles, batting them back and forth with co-authors for a couple of days before they start writing. The process of finding the best title is a way of defining exactly what the paper will be about and, in a joint writing situation, will also serve as a way of negotiating agreement on the shape of what is to come. There is nothing worse than discussing a new writing project, wandering off to write your bit and then discovering a couple of weeks (or months) later that this was not what the other person thought they had agreed to at all. Writing is hard enough without taking time-consuming detours down the cul de sac of 'I'm not sure that's what we discussed'. If you are stuck, or feeling a bit vague and suspect you may be at cross-purposes with your collaborators, then this is a great exercise (at any stage of the writing process) for getting back on the same page.

Another friend of mine uses her first sentence as a kind of bridge between all the reading and note taking she's been doing and the paper she is going to write. She hones her first sentence, spending hours if necessary, writing and rewriting it to frame her paper and signal its contribution. Once she has got that out of the way, the rest of the paper flows from there. That's a tall order for one sentence, and if you hate a blank piece of paper then it wouldn't be for you (I know I couldn't do it!), but it unlocks the whole process for her, acting as an anchor and a road sign that the rest of the paper can follow.

STORYBOARDS

When I am working with co-authors I tend to negotiate the paper with them by setting out a storyboard of what that paper will look like. This will identify the main literature that we will use, list the arguments and evidence and, crucially for joint work, who will write what. This becomes a psychological contract for the paper; an agreement between us.

This idea hails from the world of film where directors use a storyboard, a mix of words and pictures laid out a bit like a comic strip to order their ideas for their shooting of each scene and how those scenes will build to a narrative. I often use this kind of approach when I agree the 'shape' of a paper with my co-authors. It is usually one or two sides of paper with a bunch of headings and subheadings to signal the overall structure of the piece, along with some notes under each one to remind me what will go in each part and what the purpose of that part is in terms of delivering the argument of the paper. The storyboard is not written in sentences. Each section will contain a mix of diagrams, references that I need to discuss, signposts to bits of predecessor conference papers that I want to include and bullet points that cover all the main arguments. Once it is hashed out, discussed with everyone involved and rehashed, I will also add initials to each of the bits to show who has agreed to do what. This becomes the basis for our collaboration as well as the basis of the paper. It serves the same internal purpose for collaborators as a structured abstract does for the readers of the finished paper. It communicates the main thrust of the paper. However, it will be written before all the reading is done, and in the case of a qualitative piece, often before the analysis is finalised, and so it is full of gaps and inconsistencies that will need to be resolved as the writing progresses. Sometimes the section for the literature review will just be a list of questions I need to answer. For a quantitative paper I will paste in a couple of my graphs in lieu of a findings section, and for a qualitative one, a list of themes with significant quotes that represent them. There will be a list of references to show where the reading will start and some major themes described to suggest how they might be ordered in the final piece, but it is even draftier than a first draft. Way draftier. Not so much an itinerary as a compass. What you are aiming for is, 'OK everyone, let's try thataway'. And see what happens.

When I am writing on my own, or writing my bit of a paper, I do this mapping out through brainstorming headings. I open a blank file and fill it with a list of headings that I will need to fill up with words to do the work of the paper. So, on a paper on how cognitive dissonance affects the decisions people make about purchasing flights, I will need headings on cognitive dissonance, some aspects of cognitive dissonance theory that I am going to use to make my points, some literature on the pros and cons of this theory, some examples of how it has been used in similar studies, etc. I blast these headings out, moving and nesting, grouping and refining them until I have a rough 'shape' of the paper. As I read and write I add more headings or take some away to remind myself of the building blocks I am going to need to deliver my argument and join my chosen debate. This facilitates the 'writing out of order' strategy that I advocate below (see Placeholders, this section) and also is effective against the blank piece of paper syndrome.

PLACEHOLDERS

When I am writing by myself, or I have responsibility for the first draft of a piece, I don't bother with a storyboard. I just open a document and start typing headings. I put them in any old order. I will type notes under some of them like *Don't forget to mention that new thing Ken wrote* or similar. Other headings which have bits that won't be written by me will just have the person's name in them. Think more shopping list than masterplan. When I have got everything out of my head (please note, those readers who are still hoping for a systematic system to be advocated here, that I did not write, 'Once I have got some headings for every section'. If I have no immediate ideas for the discussion the heading will be: Discussion. This is about serving my process, not the paper's needs at this stage), I will have a scroll through to see if anything else occurs to me and then I might start bunching or ordering the headings a bit. Not much, just a loose or vague association. For me, writing is a pretty messy and organic process. I will often break off writing something to slap another heading in somewhere else as it occurs to me that I will need to add a section on that topic. Equally, there is no point in me spending loads of time fleshing out every subtitle or every section and deciding whether that should be 1.3.4.7 or 1.3.5.1 because, honestly, some of them are going to be deleted, shifted, expanded into massive sections and then cut out altogether to become a separate paper in their own right, or even shuffled into several different parts of the paper before I am done. Time trying to be precise at this stage is time wasted.

I collect references in a similar kind of way. When I am in the early stages of writing a new piece, or notwritingatall on an old one, all I might have is a folder on my PC with some journal articles in it that I squirrel things away in so I don't lose them. For me it is more important to have an article associated with a project than it is to have a single file saved under the author and date in a database shared by all my projects. For mammoth projects where the literature is the data (like in McDonald, Gan, Fraser, Oke & Anderson, 2015, for example), I do use a database. But if I am reading something for one purpose and it occurs to me that I will probably want to cite it in two other back-burner projects, I am likely to copy that article into both those folders (all my information management friends are cringing right now!). Sort of like a digital version of the piles of paper on the floor behind your chair. I end up with multiple copies of the articles I really like and use all the time, but I remember to read them when I am next working on that project (which, for me, can be years apart, remember! Sssslllllooooooooooowwwwwww).

Once I have a spattering of headings to mess up the blank piece of paper, I will just start writing. I scroll down, pick a heading and start to type. As I mentioned before, that is how I am writing this book. If I get stuck halfway through a sentence, I abandon it, leave it hanging and move on to type whatever is next. Sometimes I will come back to it later, but sometimes when I come back either the idea has gone or it has got itself incorporated elsewhere so I don't need it anymore. I don't necessarily write in academic language either. To begin with, I am kind of explaining the idea to myself. Just typing away, while no one is looking. Nothing to see, no big deal. Just talking to myself in Calibri …

I often begin my writing before I begin my reading in earnest. You can bet your life that once I get to nailing down a section and putting proper reference lists in it that I will read everything. Anything. In more than one discipline if nobody tries to talk me out of it. But, at that early stage, the detailed reading just slows me down and stifles what I want to say with all the polished and well-articulated arguments until I can't see my own point anymore. So I will often draft a tentative argument before I have read more than about half a dozen things in that area.

TAKE A NOTE

When I am writing, I often come across things I need to check, look up or find: a paper I think would make a good reference for the point I am making; the exact words the author or interviewee I am quoting said; a date; a name; an amount; the number of Tuesdays in 2007. I also find my train of thought interrupted by splendid ideas for something else I am writing, or tangential observations that may or may not be useful for the piece I am working on.

I have discovered that I can lose a whole half a day raking through my filing cabinet or browsing online to try to track down the exact reference I have in my mind's eye. So when that happens, I make a note in the text and add it to my 'to do' list for that paper. The note in the text might just say (ref) or it might be more expansive like (ref Weick paper on sensemaking?) or more specific like (check date), (spelling?). These act as a marker so that I don't stop and do them now, breaking my momentum and my line of thought, but I also don't forget and leave things unchecked or unreferenced. As my drafts get more formal and nearer the finished article, I highlight these inserted notes in really bright colours because I live in fear of submitting a paper with an elegant point followed by (put refs in here)! I also add the task implied by the note to my paper's 'to do' list. I have a notebook full of 'to do' lists for papers. Each one starts on a new page and keeps everything together: all the tiny things I want to check, the papers I want to read or track down and my idea for taking out a section completely. When someone cancels a meeting unexpectedly, I open my notebook and see if there is a tiny task I can do quickly before the next meeting starts.

When I feel myself getting lost in my own side arguments or find a paragraph that, although beautifully argued, does not fit into the argument I am currently trying to put together, I just take it out of the body of the paper and copy it at the end of the file on a new page. It is neither in my paper nor out of it. When I get near the end of the paper, I review these orphaned sentences, paragraphs and notes to myself to see whether they need to be written back into the paper. A friend has a similar process but he keeps his notes on paper as a list of questions to be resolved. They tend to be one of three things:

1. Something already in the paper which, although expressed beautifully, is not really necessary here. Often because it is a slightly different way of explaining something you've already explained, or the same argument but in a slightly different order. My co-author generally puts her pen through these for me because it is really hard to do it myself. 'Kill your darlings' is her philosophy. Eeeeeek! She is always right.
2. Something that ought to be in the paper but I haven't yet managed to get to fit in my argument or lie down flat. Time to go back to that section of the paper and work it in.
3. Something that belongs to a different project or turns out to be paragraph 37 of a paper you haven't even thought of writing yet. Get your notebook out, make a new page, save it in a new file all of its own and wait to see whether a paper will grow to claim it.

None of my papers get submitted until the dodgy notes lurking on the final page of my penultimate draft have been dealt with in one of these ways: out, in or in a different paper.

WRITING TO FIND OUT HOW IT WILL END

The main reason I write storyboards and not plans for my writing is the same reason that I never start writing at the beginning: narratives will change as you write. Writing has a life of its own. It is pretty badly behaved, like most creative endeavours, and does not like to be predictable or orderly in its manifestation. That paper you thought you were writing about 'The role of turquoise in organisational change'? Turns out to be 'Blue/green and green/ blue: The debates through an activity theory lens'. One of the real reasons that I can't give up on a paper once it has begun is that I need to know how it ends. The only way to find out is by writing it.

This phenomenon is well documented throughout the arts (see, for example, Hemingway, 1964; Walker, 1983; for academic studies try Taylor, Hodges & Kohányi, 2003; Foxwell, Alderson-Day, Fernyhough & Woods, 2020). Whilst some writers see this as a maddening loss of control, or evidence that they are not doing it 'properly', others read it as a sign of creativity. In qualitative research we have the wonderful excuse that we are allowing the data to speak to the reader. We are really just a kind of wordy, mortal go-between amongst the thoughts. If you think your own words and ideas are rowdy and constantly messing up your plans, you should try qualitative data: they are wild. Actually, plenty of people have had the experience of writing having a life of its own and narratives changing themselves to the extent that you begin to see yourself not as the creator of the words but as the medium through which they are expressed. Lots of civilised folks keep it to themselves in case others think they are not serious individuals with a stern grip on the facts.

If this is sometimes true at the level of writing a paper and there are days when every single paragraph seems to have an escape plan, then it is always true of a doctoral thesis. There is no way that you can start a document this size and plan out how it will end at the beginning. Most research students change their title (if not their topic) three times in their first three months of reading, even before they type a single official word of their thesis. Please don't worry about this and know that (a) it is universal. I have supervised, mentored and managed hundreds of research students and never have I ever sent a thesis away to an examiner that matched the application that that student wrote years earlier. Never. And (b) it is inevitable. You cannot know the end at the beginning. That is what it means to do research. Go with it. The place it wants to take you is better than the one you glimpsed from the end of your master's degree. You are not getting further and further away from your thesis as it shifts and changes under your very hands as you type, you are getting closer and closer.

FINDING IDEAS

It is relatively rare to be stuck at the stage of generating ideas, but just in case you really aren't inspired right now, here is how people stumbled across (you know this stuff is rarely planned, right?) the ideas for the papers they are writing. Writing projects all start in different places, although some of us do have a distinctive modus operandi when it comes to finding problems to centre on. The most common sources of ideas people shared with me were:

- Anomalies: Data that show the theory didn't work as predicted; or that demonstrate success that the theory would have ruled out. Tensions that arise between data and theory are a rich source of ideas.
- Conversations with other academics: I have papers that started out as lunchtime discussions. You don't have to have social skills or friendship circles at work to do this, though. One of the glorious side effects of writing out what we think and making it available to everyone for all time is that we can still prove, contradict or extend the work of folks who are long gone from this world. Or orchestrate an 'argument' between two folk who have never met or heard of each other.
- Crossing boundaries: Taking the tools and perspectives out of one discipline into another.
- Contributing to policy debates: What are the policy makers struggling to deal with, and how could you help?
- Contributing to practitioner debates: Are there points of contention right now in the practitioner communities you serve or research? What could your discipline's theories add to the development of solutions?
- Rage: Is something that another academic or discipline is saying or doing really beginning to rub you up the wrong way? Is there some received wisdom that always has you inwardly (hopefully) shout 'Not True' every time you come across it? Time to write a paper to put the whole thing right.

If your ideas are still uninspired then try something more inspiring. Look to art, fiction, poetry, music, film or theatre for some new perspective. Toni Morrison finds paintings can generate ideas for her books; Salman Rushdie gets fired up by watching films (Stodola, 2015). Even if you don't find a brilliant idea for a chapter of a monograph on microbiology, you will certainly cheer yourself up.

DEADLINES

Some people react very well to deadlines. Others don't. Some people who hate deadlines nevertheless seek them out with an impressive level of dedication! I'm guessing that you might not be reading this if you could solve this whole thing by setting yourself sensible deadlines and then delivering against them. On the other hand, if you haven't actually given this a go, it is definitely worth a try.

If your own deadlines don't make much of an impression, try escalating! When I write with co-authors (see Section 2, Get a co-author) I am usually much better at sticking to jointly agreed deadlines. Although, the better they know and love me, the less well this works. For some people I spoke with, the idea of being judged tardy against even their imagined notions of a co-author's expectations was enough to send them into a flurry of writing. In the same way that turning your private writing practices into public ones by talking about them with others or sharing them with co-authors can help, making deadlines public in even the smallest of ways really works for some writers. So do try saying your deadlines out loud to a writing buddy or a co-author and see whether what social scientists like to call 'public commitment' (Burn & Oskamp, 1986) works its magic for you.

If agreeing deadlines with others informally doesn't work for you, or wears off after a while, try using more external deadlines to up the ante. I often use conferences like this. It only works for conferences where you have to submit a full paper, rather than just an abstract. But the idea is that you commit to a specific conference and then you get funnelled through its deadlines, and by the time the conference comes around, you effectively have to have produced a first draft of your paper and also got some feedback. If you choose your conference wisely, you can even get some feedback that is relevant to the target journal you have in your mind's eye by choosing the annual gathering of the folks who are also associated with that journal. Lots of academic communities have both an annual conference and a strong link to a specific journal, so you can engineer a bunch of really relevant feedback for yourself.

I have a friend who uses special issues of journals in a similar way. She gets notifications for all the calls for papers for special issues of her favourite journals and then uses the vast data sets she is already sitting on to write something targeted at a particular special issue. That way she has to fall in with the timescales dictated by the journal. Hey presto: manufactured deadline! This strategy has the added benefit of shortening the wait (particularly for social scientists) between acceptance of a paper and its publication, as the timing of the special issue has often been negotiated in advance by its editors.

SPEED

I am a slow writer. Veeeerrrrry slow. Slower than whatever you just imagined when you read 'veeeeerrrry slow'. I have always understood this as a negative aspect of my practice. One science scholar I spoke with told me that in every experimental procedure there is a 'rate-determining' factor. In almost any writing partnership I've ever had, that factor is me! However, I am coming to understand that writing only moves at a certain pace.[5] One way that you can fool yourself into thinking that you are writing 'more' is to churn out large volumes of words. Cover pages, rack up word counts. It definitely looks like the folks who can dash off thousands of words in a day are writing more than me. What I have learned is that these bursts of writing are often either edited down dramatically (or scrapped altogether) or the successful writing time is followed by 'fallow' days which don't yield anything productive at all. Another version of this is writers who draft and redraft whole documents dozens of times before they ever see the light of day. Although my iterations are slower they are relatively few compared with others. I will only have four to six completely revised versions of a paper from start to finish. In other words, whether you write massive, rangy drafts that you will later cull or write and rewrite each sentence, there's probably not as much difference between the rate of output of finished text per hour as it might first appear.

WRITING FOR FOUR HOURS EACH DAY

Over the years I have found that I can only write for about four hours each day, and certainly never more than six. On the days that I write for longer I am usually (a) writing hell for leather under imminent threat of a deadline (a real, last-chance-or-you'll-blow-the-whole-thing deadline with a ring in its nose and sleeve tattoo, not one of those nice, polite ones with a clipboard that people invent to fool themselves into writing because it would be nice to have it finished by Thursday) and/or (b) gathering up all the unwritten words from the last two weeks of stuck and adding most of tomorrow's words too. Actually, the notion of only writing a certain amount of words or for a certain amount of time is something that is generally accepted by many writers of fiction (King, 2000; see also Pang, 2016 for an impressive list of creatives with four hour work days). I suggest that if, like me, you write very slowly that you aim to write for a specific period each day rather than trying to focus on a number of words (see Goals in this section).

I think that the reason for this, particularly for academic writing, is that novel, complex or difficult ideas take a certain amount of processing time. So whether you force yourself to sit at the computer for nine hours straight or go for a walk after three, you can't get through a cycle of the reading process to the thinking process to the writing process any faster. Writing can only move at the speed of your capacity for deep processing. Staring at it or threatening yourself won't help. The only possible way to speed myself up is to show someone else a draft or, even better in my case, to talk it through. My speaking brain is a powerful and more immediate sensemaker which I find can travel faster than my writing brain (see Section 2, Get a writing buddy).

ROUTINES

I use this term because I think it is better than 'habits'. For me, habits are time and space bound. They are done mindlessly. They have bypassed our thinking brain and rest in our muscle memory. Like brushing your teeth. Have you ever driven to work and suddenly noticed that you haven't noticed that last 10 miles? That is the power of habit. It is really powerful but not, in my view, what is wanted here. What we need to support our writing is routine.

Some people like to write in the same place. They like to have everything at hand and know that they don't need any phaffing-about time. They have the perfect set up where they can just sit down and write. It is their way of reducing barriers.

Another routine element to try is having some writing music. If you are the sort of person who did their school homework listening to the radio or who takes a soundtrack to the gym, then this could be a really useful tool. You need to choose wisely, though. Tracks with catchy (or meaningful) lyrics or those that trigger strong emotions are not that helpful. This is not writing music: save those tracks for your dancing in the kitchen! What I am saying is: don't choose your favourite song. Choose something you can put in the background and train yourself not to hear. This is not about music appreciation; it is more akin to a form of self-hypnosis. Some people pick a tune that they only play while they are writing. This triggers a Pavlovian response[6] in their brains: after a while, hearing the music triggers their writing. Although this is not my bag, I can testify to the power of suggestion music can have on your brain. When I hear 'The Only Way is Up' by Yazz and the Plastic Population, I get an unmistakable urge to do grapevines courtesy of 1980s aerobics classes in the sports centre of my alma mater.

If you either prefer to write in lots of different places, don't have a writing space that you can maintain or regularly work on the train or in airports then having some writing music up your sleeve can be especially useful because it makes your 'writing space' aural and therefore portable. You can access it wherever you are and shortcut to progress however odd the space you find yourself in might be. It can also drown out all the distracting noises in a place to let you focus on your writing.

One settling routine I can recommend is switching off notifications. All those wee red circles and pings. Go through your settings and switch them all off. If you cannot have them off all the time, you might need to change them at the start of your writing session. Sometimes, closing certain apps or programs (like your email or calendar) can have a big impact without much effort. Some people use a different computer to write than they use the rest of the time. I have a friend with a PC dedicated to her creative work which sits in a different room to her work computer and is not connected to the internet. This way she can guarantee not being interrupted and there is no need to go through her settings switching stuff off every time she wants to concentrate on her artwork. This might seem like a trivial suggestion, but it serves a great practical purpose (reducing your interruptions and potential distractions) at the same time as sending a message to yourself and to the rest of the world that your writing time has begun. Crucially, this signals a change in our underlying assumptions about who is making the decisions over how our time is spent. If we react to every email notification, then we are placing our time and priority management into the hands of others. Many of us have developed a Pavlovian response to the electronic beeps of our communication and social media software which has us convert our attention on demand to whatever others are saying or asking us to do. Switching off notifications allows us to take back control of our time and priorities and signals to ourselves the importance of our writing within our day. See Section 6 for some suggestions of software that can do that for you!

Over time, these practical routines and settling techniques can help us develop a new Pavlovian response, reducing the barriers and resistance to starting to write and helping support our intentions with some automatic writing behaviours.

WRITING OUT LOUD

I am a talker. Anyone who knows me (actually, anyone who has ever met me) will verify this. I talk a LOT. An awful lot! So I really don't know why it took me such a very long time to work out that my natural proclivity for talk might be something that might help my notwriting. Funny how we are often hell bent on working against ourselves instead of harnessing the talents we already know we have. Maybe it was because throughout school I was not necessarily encouraged to think of my constant yapping as a gift. Anyway. Turns out talking is my sensemaking superpower.

I have two different versions of writing out loud that help me get unstuck. The first is to clutch the recalcitrant manuscript in one hand and go in search of an unsuspecting colleague to help me berate it. Now I have been spoilt because I have worked in the same building as some really cool people. People with writing reputations so large that they are generous in their tolerance of other people's writing puzzles and/or people with hearts so kind that they wouldn't dream of turning away a colleague in need of a rant. So many of the papers that I have written have been ironed out in the process of a 10 minute conversation with someone else. At least half the time, I have suggested my own solution two minutes into my own tirade about how this paper is badly behaved and just won't lie down flat. This works a bit like the rubber duck in Section 2, Get a rubber duck.

Somehow, talking activates a different process in my brain and, in my own explanation of the problem, I can suddenly see a solution. I am sure there is an actual scientific explanation for this, but you won't hear it from me. Just trust me and give it a shot. When it works, it is the shortest way to catapult yourself from notwriting to writing, often for nothing more than the cost of a gifted cappuccino. In my view, this is why we have staff common rooms. They provide places to lurk with your half-eaten drafts and wait for folk to wave them at whilst they check their pigeon holes for post. (Sigh. Those were the days …)

The other version is for days when you have tried loads of other things and you are still notwriting, verging on NOTwriting. Or for folks where the composing isn't hard, but the actual, physical act of typing is a taxing process. Try using a Dictaphone or voice-recording app to talk out your ideas. There are now automatic online transcription services that you can load your audio on to and get a print version back. The quality isn't brilliant, and it takes them a while to get used to voices, like mine, which have a regional accent, but if you are really stuck then correcting words might be a lot easier to get going with than composing words. If you plan to do this a lot you could invest in dictation software which types as you talk. I used this when I suffered from carpal tunnel syndrome and couldn't type for a few months. It is worth checking if your university has a license: many do now as part of their accessibility support for folks with dyslexia and other interesting challenges. Or you can pay for an actual person to do your transcription. These are excellent quality but also pretty expensive. If you are going to transcribe yourself then I suggest dictating in short sections so that your notwriting doesn't turn into NOTtranscribing. I often find that I don't need more than a couple of sections dictated like this before I can start writing again.

If talking is not your superpower, is there something else that is? Do you draw a wicked diagram? Can you make scintillating presentations? Are you a flowchart ninja? Rather than starting with a spoken draft of your writing, you could start with a picture, a schemata, a spreadsheet, a doodle, a slide deck, a mind map. The first draft, especially at storyboard level, does not need to be in the form of continuous prose. Try some other format to unlock the shape of what you want and see whether the leap from there to words is easier than from a blank page.

A note for those with any condition that makes either physically typing or cognitively transferring the glorious thing in your head into actual characters on a page another level of difficult:

1. Respect.
2. You are not slow. You are probably not notwriting. Even if you are notwriting you are also battling your condition. See 1 above.
3. I want you to know that I know at least two BRILLIANT, senior academics who share your battle. Their writing is both excellent and prolific. I know several folks with PhDs who were not diagnosed until they were a year or so into their doctorate. It can be done. See 1 above.

4. Please get some support with this. You don't have to (a) pretend not to have your condition or (b) solve the problems it causes all by yourself. Tell people. Ask for what you need to make the playing field level. Also see 1 above.

There are also some places to start noted in Section 6.

LOWER YOUR STANDARDS

In Section 3 you'll find some words of wisdom from a recovering perfectionist (see Perfectionism). The antidote to perfectionism is to lower your standards. We've already noted that reducing the amount you plan to write in each stint is important (see Goals in this section), but for some folks there is another part to that story: as well as writing less, you need to learn to write less well. Although we will all need to write splendid things eventually, there is no need to write splendidly from the start. Save splendid for another draft on another day and just begin. The job of the first draft is not to do anything but stop the page being blank. So, scribble some notes or type in some bullets and add some random ideas and give yourself something to edit another day. Editing is easier to approach and easier to begin than writing, so your future self will definitely thank you for some words to improve upon rather than starting with a blank page. See Drafts in this section. Also, have a look at Section 3, Writing is a single skill: this is a misconception at best and a massive road block at worst.

BLOCKS OF TIME AND BLOCKING OUT TIME

In other parts of this book I will try to persuade you that we don't need great expanses of time in which to write (see Section 3, Enough time). Most things can be written in a series of half hour or 20 minute slots if you keep this going as a daily practice. However, lots of folks I spoke with liked to block out writing time (see also Evans & Smith, 2019). Most of them favoured either two or four hour blocks for this. The interesting thing was that they booked these times in their diaries in advance. At the beginning of a week or a month or a semester they would look ahead and assign specific times for writing and put them in their diaries as a meeting with themselves. Some went on to 'agree' these with a co-author. Honestly, if I did this, I would quickly realise that the sum of the spaces does not add up to the time required for the draft book chapter I'm supposed to be working on (perhaps this is why I don't do it!). As well as feeling that some time slots were too short for writing (not everyone likes my 20 to 30 minute slots, for example), some people felt that some time slots (whole days, for example) were too long for writing because they would run out of steam in the afternoon. Rather than creating unsatisfactory time slots which they already knew would not serve their own idiosyncrasies, they had found the perfect length of time for them and that's what they booked in their diaries. If, like me, you have always written under the imminent pressure of a crazy deadline, and you don't know what length of time is actually most productive for you (or even how much you write in a 'normal' hour), you could experiment with some time blocks in your diary over the next week or month and see what suits you.

WRITE PLACE

We tell ourselves that we need to be in the right place to write. This can look like a belief about being in the right (or right kind of) physical place. Plenty of people treat their inspiration as a fragile, fleeting thing that will only appear under certain, very specific, conditions. In a particular room of your house, seat in the library, table in the coffee shop. There are plenty of academics who tell me that they can't work in the office because there are people there and if they get interrupted once their flow will be broken and that will be the end of their writing for the day.

This can also look like a belief about being in the right frame of mind. Some of us believe we can only write when we are in a happy place. Others love the idea of tormented souls à la Brontë sisters. You don't need to be in a good mood to write. Believe me: I once wrote a whole paper over a single weekend in a fit of spite. Guess which one, if you like.

Listening to some folk talk about the conditions which must be met before they can write is a bit like reading a medieval love spell: only if the dew of the grass on the eastern meadow is drunk at the exact moment of dawn on the third Thursday in June … Honestly, we all need our rituals (see Routines in this section), but all of this just speaks to me of superstition, scarcity and fear. Most of this is limiting thinking which helps excuse us from being able to write most of the time. If you are feeling superstitious about your writing, try to gradually relax about it to allow yourself more latitude. Do you need your lucky socks, or is it really just that you find it hard to write if your feet are cold? Does it have to be that table in the library, or would any one with a wee view of the trees be fine? Be gentle with yourself. We set up these complex If/Then/Else conditions because we are worried. Don't wipe them all out with a single stroke of brave new worldness. Unpick them quietly and cheer yourself on as you widen your options until you get to a place where you can write comfortably in a realistic range of settings and moods.

CHANGING PLACE

One of the most effective ways for me to re-engage with a project is to change my writing setting. When I am really stuck I take myself out of my office. If I am at work I go to a café or other public circulation area and set myself up at an empty table to write. If I am at home I leave my study and sit at the kitchen table, or even outside (on the three days in Scotland when this is possible) instead. Or I walk up through the village and buy my draft some lunch. Like small children, drafts are sometimes better behaved in public. My favourite place to work is on a train. Not on short, noisy, crowded commuter journeys, but travelling to meetings at other universities. I discovered this by always having last-minute work to do for the meeting I am travelling to join. I try to book a seat in the quiet coach and I get an astonishing amount of work done over the course of a journey. I now deliberately take trains to other parts of the country and factor in the journey as a deadline to have a piece of work ready to redraft. Hotel rooms are another massively productive place for writing for me. I have lots of colleagues who have tiny laptops so that they can take their papers out of the office. However, I also like to set up a rhythm where I type things at my desk and then print out drafts and take them out of the office to redraft with a pen. Then back to the office to type. When I mark up a draft on the train I often type it up in my hotel room. For me, a trip away for work brings the opportunity to completely redraft a paper. In fact, when I grind to a halt on a project one of my long-standing (long-suffering?) co-authors sometimes wonders aloud when I am next going to be on a train. Funnily enough, I don't find air travel productive in this way. I often read a lot on a flight, but don't find either aeroplanes or airports conducive for writing.

The café trick is one that I found well used amongst the colleagues that I interviewed. It has been made famous by J. K. Rowling, who wrote the Harry Potter books in Edinburgh cafés and completed the last one in a hotel room. I don't know why it works. Sometimes I think it is the panopticon effect. A panopticon is a building designed so that those in authority can observe everyone not in authority without those poor souls being certain exactly when they are being observed. It was posited by Jeremy Bentham as a way to design hospitals, schools or, more famously, prisons, to increase compliance with social rules (Fontana-Giusti, 2013). Foucault (a French philosopher) uses it as a metaphor for how society works to make us conform. Here I mean simply this: if you set out your writing in a public place then you had better be seen to be writing. This idea of being seen being productive in itself is somewhat undermined by the vast amount of research showing that open-plan office spaces are not conducive to tasks that need creativity or concentration (see Section 5, Open-plan offices). It could be that the pleasant noise and chatter of others' leisure makes for a creative backdrop or a sense of community that puts us at ease. Perhaps it is simply a literally new perspective. It is possible that we feel invisible and confident that we won't be disturbed. Maybe the coffee helps. Or given that it works when I move from one room in my house to another, and that trains are so productive for me, perhaps it is the movement itself.

If you don't know what your favourite writing places might be, or if you have always written in the office or at a desk at home, I suggest some experiments next time you are stuck. I have written some of this book in my study at home, mostly in the afternoons, but sometimes in the dead of night (which is another place) but over the years I have been writing it I have also worked on it:

- in cafés, with a hot chocolate to hand (in my village, in art galleries, at work, in museums, at other universities);
- in my mum's house, when she was away on holiday;
- in the car outside the swimming pool, waiting for lessons to end;
- in hotel rooms, so many different hotel rooms;
- in empty conference rooms at work;
- in restaurants after dinner when I have been travelling alone;
- on so many trains that sometimes I wish I'd counted the miles of writing instead of the minutes or pages;
- at the kitchen table;
- in libraries (university and civilian);
- parked at the beach with a view of the sea;
- between sessions at conferences;
- and even, once or twice, in my office at work.

You can't do all the different things that 'writing' entails in every sort of place (see Section 3, Writing is a single skill), but there is work you can do in any place you feel settled for an hour. Please don't mistake this for permission or persuasion that you should take your writing everywhere with you, or try to cram it into every moment of your life. Quite the opposite: it is an invitation to consider moving someplace else with your writing and plan to write there for a specific time to see whether that helps. As a rule of thumb: the more stuck I am, the less traditional a writing setting I need to get unstuck.

One of the most blissful things about writing is that it is something you can do alone. However, this also means that if you don't do it then it will not get done. Throw into the mix that for academics nobody can see whether you are writing or not writing and no one will be able to tell whether you wrote or did not write on a specific day until months afterwards, when it becomes apparent that you must not have been writing on any of the days and you have the perfect recipe for (a) notwriting and (b) hopelessly damaging your faith in your ability to write and (c) feeding a towering guilt storm about notwriting. One way to break into this charming cycle is to be seen writing. For me this means writing in public places. It is my attempt to invoke the gaze of the panopticon gaoler upon myself as a means of self-discipline (Fontana-Giusti, 2013).

HANDWRITING

It's funny how we still speak about 'writing' when so often we are typing now-adays. I am old enough to remember handwritten drafts and to know people who wrote their theses and books by hand and gave them to a typist. I am from the first generation who typed their own theses on PCs with black screens and green phosphor type, DOS-based bibliometric databases and striped printouts with holes up the side. So perhaps it is because there is a comfort and familiar-ity in handwriting for my age group and that this will be different for younger writers, but give it a try. Writing with pen on paper gives you a different con-nection to what you are writing. For me there is a flow in writing that doesn't come with typing. It feels more immediate and less formal. Handwriting on drafts is particularly powerful for me. Even if you don't handwrite or edit your drafts, I would definitely try to introduce handwriting to increase your connection and creativity. I implore my doctoral students to keep a hardback notebook full of analytical thoughts.

CHANGE OF PROJECT

One of the things I did when I was researching this book was deliberately interview prolific writers. I figured that they had got this whole writing thing sorted out and I wanted to know what their advice was for the rest of us poor, struggling mortals. One of the most surprising findings was that they all got stuck. They recognised the phenomenon immediately and confessed that they regularly met this in their writing. I am not sure whether to offer this to you as a heartening or discouraging revelation, but there it is. Everyone gets stuck. The difference is that they:

1. recognised the stuck;
2. did not panic about being stuck;
3. did not allow themselves to stay stuck for any length of time; and
4. had strategies for getting unstuck.

And do you know what the top strategy was for getting unstuck? The most common approach was to put down the thing they were stuck on after as little as 10 minutes of stuck (I know!) and change to working on another project.

Some people have the perception that having multiple writing projects in various states of unfinishedness is just disorganisation, a lack of focus or that it is dividing up the very small amount of time we have to write into smaller and smaller pieces. But lots of people find it energising and enabling (what shall I write today?) and it is key for many folks, as a way of making sure they don't ever *stay* stuck. Interestingly, even the people who told me that they definitely only wrote one thing at a time generally went on to describe the many things they had in progress at various stages of development. The real difference between those who seemed stuck and those who did not was that those who were stuck described the multiple projects as a problem, whereas those who did not get stuck (or rather stay stuck) perceived this same thing as a writing strategy.

I find this strategy a bit alien if I am honest. To put down a paper and pick up a book chapter on something else feels too fast and daring to me. But I do a mini version of it with my flitting between headings. If I am stuck on a section, I simply move on to type in another section that catches my eye (as outlined in Placeholders in this section). So now you know. The top writing strategy is to have loads of projects on the go, don't allow yourself to be stuck for even a whole hour and simply change projects if one of them is sulking. Try it!

LETTING IT GO COLD

Running underneath a lot of the tactics I suggest is that when you are stuck, what you need is a new perspective. If you haven't got people you can share your writing with, or ask for feedback, then one way to get a brand new perspective on something you are stuck with is to stop wrestling with it and let it go cold. This entails deliberately deciding to put the project down for a while. Sometimes sleeping on it is enough to get some new perspective. Sometimes it will need a few weeks or even a couple of months to look different. While it might be tempting to use this as the perfect excuse to not write anything for a while, many of the most productive writers I spoke to favoured picking up another writing project instead. In fact, in some cases it was exactly this practice that led them to have several writing projects in hand at any one time (see Change of project in this section). I think this is a key reason that it is hard to write quickly: you can only go as fast as the thinking, and that needs periods of 'wintering' to support new growth. See Speed in this section.

The point of this is that it is not the same as procrastination. Procrastination is a strategy where you are supposed to be doing something you are not doing. Or when you get really good at it, it can look like doing something else that is more urgent (but less important) than the thing you ought to be doing: whole careers in academic management have been forged in just this way! The subtle difference here is that you are giving yourself permission not to write it (see Permission slips in this section). Quite different from notwriting, where you are just avoiding the thing.

One of the miracles of the human brain is that you may find, on returning to your stone-cold writing problem, that your mind has been working on it while you were working on other projects and it has figured out a solution. Doing something else has stopped progress on this project but it has not slowed your writing progress overall. It might even speed you up. You have created slack in the system for your brain to produce a more creative (and definitely more pleasant) outcome than you could ever have produced by staring at it for days and/or beating yourself up about it.

NEVER LET A DAY GO PAST

One of the most prolific writers interviewed for this study was once asked by a junior colleague in a seminar on writing what his secret was. He said that his top advice was to always keep your research in motion and never let a day go past when you did not do something, however small, to advance something you were working on. Sometimes, he said, at the end of a long day teaching and being in endless meetings, as he put his coat on to leave his office he would spend 10 minutes fishing a specific paper out of his filing cabinet. He would put the paper on his desk before he left so that it was there, ready for him to read in the morning. It only took 10 minutes, but it was all he had the energy and headspace for at the end of a day bursting with other demands and, even though it was tiny and insignificant, it was still travel in the right direction. Progress.

This particular colleague had a seven-day-a-week writing habit, which for most of us is neither sustainable nor desirable, so he quite literally 'never let a day go past'. A more sensible, realistic and healthy version of that would be to 'never let a work day go past'. Always forward. Sometimes just by inches, but forward, nevertheless.

There is a whole lot written about academic writing which basically boils down to: write daily. It's good advice and certainly something to try as an approach if you haven't tried it yet. Personally, I think that the size of your goals is the part of daily writing that is more powerful than the actual dailyness of it, but it definitely works for some people. I worry that daily writing is a habit just waiting to be broken by illness, babies, travel, marking, special issues and being asked to teach for an absent colleague tomorrow. In other words, it is a bandwagon waiting to be fallen off and, like a strict diet, a breeding ground for guilt and recrimination. To promise myself (my beautifully inconsistent, rebel, variety-seeking self) that I will write daily is to invite disaster. But if you hold this idea lightly and kindly it can be really powerful. For me, it works like a charm for several weeks if I try to write five or six days out of seven and keep the times short (20 minutes when I am stuck; up to an hour when I am in flow) and I can produce an astonishing amount of words which quietly pile up on top of each other into whole drafts. Plus, I get the giddy feeling of believing myself to be an actual adult for a wee while, which, you know, is not to be underestimated. But I also find that although I can do this consistently over quite long periods sometimes, I can never do it forever. The streak of productivity is, for me at least, always accompanied by streaks of fallow. I used to beat myself up about this and also spend the productive days with white knuckles as I braced myself for failure tomorrow, but now I have learned to accept these cycles and thus enjoy the heady days of feeling in control of my destiny when I am writing every day and forgive the fallow.

~~CHOCOLATE~~ REWARDS

When you do write (and you will write, I promise), you need to reward yourself, especially at the start. As well as planning your writing times, the times when you will not write and breaks, you can also plan your rewards. Plan to write all morning with some sensible breaks scheduled in and then treat yourself in some small way. Now for me this idea is inextricably linked with food. (I know. But if you want advice on the whole fewer calories thing then find another book. This one right here deals with more words.) I understand (theoretically, rather than experientially) that there are other ways to reward oneself than with chocolate. Some perfectly good people I know see reading a magazine, buying a new pen, doing a sudoku, having a bath or even running round the village as a reward. The point is: pick something you personally find (not *should* find) joyful and indulge for a moment. Focus on your achievement and, as you reward yourself, know that you are rewiring your brain for writing success.

Rewards should be in proportion to the difficulty of doing the writing rather than the number of words written. So, if you have been putting off finalising the title of your paper for two months and you have spent two hours forcing yourself to work through the alternatives and eventually committed to the seven to ten words that describe your masterpiece perfectly, you get a big reward. A whole bar. Or a new novel to download, you know, if you are not on the calories = reward thing with the rest of us mortals.

PHYSICAL ACTIVITY

When we analyse qualitative data what we need is an iterative cycle of immersion and distance. We need to get right into the heart of the data and marvel at every detail and then we need to get high up in a helicopter and scout for patterns. For me, cycles of closeness and distance are also at the heart of my writing practice. Now closeness is not always easy to achieve (see Section 3, Resistance) but at least it is obvious how one *would* do that. You would sit at your writing practice for extended periods of time and work intensively on understanding the views of other writers and of incrementally improving the clarity of your own. This is the image that we have of writing in our heads (or at least what it should look like, or definitely looks like when other people do it!). It isn't so easy to manufacture distance. You can leave your manuscript on your desk without looking at it for a couple of months (see Letting it go cold in this section), but when you are in a hurry, this is not always an option. Feedback is another way of creating a new perspective (see Section 4, Feedback), if you have a good bunch of folks around you that can oblige. However, if you have no time for the draft to grow cold and no one at hand to consult, then I suggest that the fastest and most creative route available to you is physical activity.

Amongst the folk I spoke to about being stuck, many people who were not stuck for long had a shortlist of things they habitually used to free themselves and a lot of those involved physical activity. Walking is my favourite and is used by quite a lot of people (some of whom take their dogs), but other suggestions included cycling, gardening, cleaning and the less energetic, but equally effective, getting up and making a cup of tea. Bernardo Atxaga recommends household chores like doing the laundry: 'at least the family will be pleased' (Gunesekera & Kennedy, 2015, p. 87).

CREATIVITY

I want to start by saying that I believe that academic writing is a creative process. Lots of us brush off our theses and book chapters and journal articles and even lectures as notproperwriting. As if the act of conjuring sentences only counts as a creative pursuit if the subject of that writing is fictional. Like the words can somehow tell the difference between what is real and what is not, what is written for entertainment and what is written to inform or debate. Whatever the content or purpose of your writing might be, the process is a creative one. Some of us are terrified by that as an idea; some of us are delighted. The writing is still a creative process whether you would like to think of it as one or not (I see you, the scientists pretending that you are recording immutable facts: still creative!). I personally spent most of my writing career in denial that I was a writer, caught between my resistance to acknowledge my sentences as 'real' writing and my desperate wish to be taken seriously as an academic (which is obviously a much less frivolous pastime than being a writer). I kept on being a writer regardless.

If it is true that academic writing is a creative pursuit, then this offers us another interesting avenue for getting unstuck. If you are stuck in a creative endeavour, try being creative. If the words won't come you could try drawing a diagram, sketching a schema, painting a picture. Or go oral: try talking it through, or making a presentation (see Writing out loud in this section). There is more than one artistic approach to the same thing, you will find.

What really helps me, though, is not to try to express the argument in a different medium, but to close down my writing project and do something else creative altogether. I dabble in all kinds of artistic pursuits from patchwork to land art. Even just practising the piano (which is only just barely creative in my case) or cooking something interesting helps dislodge the words stuck in my brain. I have talked already about dancing in the kitchen (the perfect juxtaposition of creative self-expression and physical exercise). If you have a few days go by without feeling inspired, try inspiring yourself by making something. Engaging in the creative process in an unrelated form, on a completely different project, is really effective for me. If you don't know how to do any arty or crafty things then you should learn. Join a class. Ask a friend. Look for an online tutorial. Try to remember the things you loved when you were little. The point is not to take on a new, expensive, time-consuming hobby that you will work on for years until you become proficient at it. The idea is just to play at something, try it out. Enjoy yourself. Make a mess. Julia Cameron's *Artist's Way* asks writers to formalise this by taking an hour every week to do something creatively challenging (Cameron, 1995). It is certainly better than spending an hour staring at your screen, even if it turns out to be unproductive. You will cheer yourself up even if you don't get yourself unstuck!

BREAKS

Taking breaks (the kind with a cup of tea, not the kind with hurling jam jars at a wall, although, you know, whatever works) is always important. However, it is important to be slightly suspicious of your break-taking strategy. Ask yourself honestly: is this a break from writing activity which is recharging my batteries and letting my thoughts settle; or could it be that choosing to buy coffee from a place at the other end of campus or wandering aimlessly round the library with a growing sense of unease is actually a mini avoidance strategy? Only you know the truth. And some of each is absolutely fine. Chances are, though, that if you have to change your electronic calendar to 'year' view to measure the length of your breaks rather than glancing at your office clock, then you need to suspect yourself of avoidance.

It's difficult. Without breaks there will be no writing. Or no sustainable writing. But too many breaks means not enough writing. I think the best way to keep yourself honest is to plan breaks. At the beginning of your writing, set yourself a time target to both write and not write. So, 'I am going to edit page 4 for 30 minutes and then I am going to nip down for a cuppa and take it back to my desk. Then I will type for another 30 minutes and then I am going to meet Cynthia for lunch for half an hour.' Plan a couple of breaks ahead and make legitimate time to do a circuit of the campus, sit outside, meditate, call your friend, colour in or do star jumps. Even if your writing day is broken up for you by lectures, meetings or video calls, make time for actual downtime as well as just being away from your writing.

Let me tell you a story. Once, when I was an undergraduate (when the stuck began), I was standing in the middle of my room frowning when my friend knocked on my door:

Friend:	I'm going for a walk, do you want to come?
Seonaidh:	No thanks, I've got an exam tomorrow. [being sure to keep up the frowning]
Friend:	Are you revising? [looking at the pile of closed books on my desk, several feet away from where I am frowning]
Seonaidh:	…
Friend:	Are you OK? [looking at the frowning]
Seonaidh:	…
Friend:	Are you going to revise?
Seonaidh:	No. I can't seem to stop this frowning and sit down next to the books with the revision in them.
Friend:	OK: Either revise; or don't revise. But standing there using up shitloads of energy frowning at those books is notrevising. Notrevising means you don't get either the benefit of the revising (knowing actual things about economics) or the benefit of not doing any revising (getting an early night or some fresh air and feeling well rested for the exam tomorrow). Instead, you use up all your energy notrevising, don't know any actual things and are also exhausted. Put your coat on, we are going for a walk.
Sconaidh:	[has epiphany, gets coat]

Here is the moral of the tale: if you take time off but do not give yourself permission to have that time off you will get no benefit (or even get negative benefit) from having that time off. Time to write yourself a permission slip and get outside. Read on for more on breaks and also check out the Permission slips in this section.

HOW TO TAKE A BREAK FOR BEGINNERS

The key thing here is that the breaks need to be legitimate, or they will not do their work in providing breakness. See the Permission slips in this section. I am pretty good at notwriting, as discussed throughout. Notwriting is not the same as a break. It is just stopping. Or even just slowing down to the extent that the speed at which you are 'writing' is not actually apparent to the human eye. But even though you may be sitting absolutely still, and even though your eyes may be closed, you are not resting. You are just directing all of your thoughts and energy into the internal battle that is notwriting. This is not restful. In fact, I find it to be the opposite of restful.

Taking breaks is not one of my earthly talents. I am a flat-out (as in running) or flat-out (as in sleeping) kinda girl. The truth is that when I am writing in a chaotic way, I am afraid to take a break from the writing because I am scared that the writing will have gone by the time I get back from my break and I will face another three days of notwriting before I get back in flow. I am also not prepared to take a break from the notwriting because I don't feel like I deserve one. So, I use my stubbornness (which definitely *is* one of my talents) to make myself sit next to the thing I am notwriting, engaging all my considerable mind power and energy to frown at it. Both of these approaches have absolutely nothing to recommend them. You can trust me on this, because, having discovered their lack of efficacy at an early age, I stubbornly (told you!) tried them over and over and over again for many years until I made myself so ill I didn't have the energy or focus to keep them up and had to think of a new strategy.

Over the years I have developed all kinds of clever ways to convince myself that I am having a break from my writing. I often gather all the notwriting up into my head and then take it into a different room. This takes me away from the actual document, but not from the notwriting. This is not a break. It can lead to a break if you are able to notice that you are still notwriting and stop focusing on it. If you were a cartoon character, you would still have a wee black cloud over your head though. Not. A. Break.

Another deception I like to practise is 'running errands'. For example, if I am using a timer to structure my writing and break times I will sit nicely and type in the writing time and then reset the timer for my break. I wander through to the kitchen to boil the kettle for a cup of tea. While the kettle is boiling I start to feel the satisfaction of having completed a writing stint but, almost immediately, my eye is caught by one of the other, eleventy billion[7] things I have not done and I think, 'I could just put some dishes away while the kettle boils'. I start to race the kettle with my endless list of tiny chores (my tea is too hot to drink just yet, I could just …). My end-of-break timer goes off and I have done loads of teeny thingsthatneeddoing but have I had a break? No. I have not. This is not a break. Nor is the work equivalent (I'll just answer this email …; I'll just have a quick look for that reference …; I'll just fish out that student email …; I'll just pop in to see if the Dean is free …). This might feel superefficient, and in the short run it may well be, but it is uncharging, not recharging your battery, thus leaving you less and not more able to write: Not. A. Break.

If you have mentally ruled out all of your usual 'break' activities whilst reading the last few paragraphs and are at a loss as to what else to try, have a look at a cat. Cats are supreme takers of breaks. You could learn a lot. As a rule of thumb, if you wouldn't catch a cat doing it, it does not qualify as a break. Emailing? Nope. Sitting in the sun? Yes. Hanging out washing? Nope. Wandering round the garden? Yes. Stretching? Yes. Eating only what is delicious? Definite yes!

Look, I realise this can be hard. We are not all natural break takers. Take it slowly. Practise. It is worth getting good at because it makes writing sustainable over the day, over the months, over your career. Just try it. If you get really good at this and get so wrapped up in the break that you forget to get back to the writing, see Sharpening pencils in this section.

PERMISSION SLIPS

The idea of giving yourself permission to do things is a powerful one and, if you find it useful in the context of learning to take breaks, you should consider trying it out in some other aspects of writing. There are all kinds of crazy things we could give ourselves permission to do that can transform our experience of writing (and life). This book suggests a few areas where we could give ourselves permission that might free up our writing. We could give ourselves permission to write stuff that isn't perfect. To write rubbish first drafts. Or permission to put our writing first. Permission to switch off our email. Permission to ask for help or support. Permission to think of ourselves as creatives.

I give myself permission to …

What are all the ways you could finish that sentence? Brainstorm a few. Come on, try a few more. Be radical. What would be a game changer for your writing? For me, it is often quite fundamental things that make the biggest difference to my writing in the end. I give myself permission to prioritise my health. To be kind to myself.

Brené Brown writes about permission slips in her books *Braving the Wilderness* (2017) and *Dare to Lead* (2018). She is an advocate of physically writing yourself a permission slip, a bit like those our parents signed and returned to school to allow us to participate in field trips and after-school activities. She writes them on slips of paper at the start of the day and puts them in her pockets. What will you write?

LAST WORD

All of these are good ideas. All of them help some people get unstuck. Not all of them will help you. Not all of those that help you will work every time you are stuck. I will, however, guarantee you one thing: none of them will get you unstuck if you leave them here, on this page. You need to give them a shot. In the same way that printing out articles and carrying them around or filing them in a pile on your desk is not the same as reading, reading these suggestions and thinking 'that's a good idea' is not the same as getting unstuck.

Getting unstuck is always a combination of trying new things, getting support and shifting your thinking. All of that can be hard. All of it takes practice. But none of it is as hard as being stuck. So you've got nothing to lose.

You don't need to do this by yourself, but there are things you can do right now, without involving anyone else.

Just start.

Right now.

Yes, 'now' now. Put down the book and try something. I've got my pom poms ready.

Try to remember

It is not just you!

We all get stuck

We all get rejections

Academic writing is hard

The system we are part of makes it harder

NOTES

1. Maurits Cornelis Escher is an artist from the Netherlands who drew mind-bending blends of maths and art, including some pretty amazing lithographs of staircases that appear to be going up and down at the same time.
2. Or maybe that should be 'by the same Tolkien', who apparently wrote the *Lord of the Rings* trilogy as a way to avoid his academic writing (Bowers, 2019).

3. See Glossary entry on Border Agency.
4. See Glossary entry on Journal lists.
5. Books, in particular, don't like to be written quickly.
6. Pavlov is the chap who conditioned dogs by feeding them every time he rang a bell. Eventually, the dogs would salivate when the bell rang even if no food was offered.
7. This number is fictional and belongs to the marvellous Gill Sims (2017).

2. Seek out support

Writing is something we tend to do on our own. So, although we have plenty of ideas about how other folks do it (easily! in a disciplined fashion!), we haven't actually witnessed anyone else's writing practice. We assume that we are the only ones who struggle and we are ashamed to talk about what we really do. For many people, especially those who are no longer 'beginners', writing practice has become a bit of a taboo subject. This unwillingness to talk about what (not)writing feels and looks like writing leads to isolation and cuts us off from the people who can help us. Add on the divisive, competitive atmosphere many academics find themselves operating within and we have the perfect recipe for (a) growing and (b) failing to tackle our fears about writing. Plus, the tone of some of the books about how to do academic writing make us feel more, rather than less, shame filled when we are stuck.

Talking to other people about being stuck with your writing is really important. First of all, it will help you to access the realisation that everyone gets stuck (of course, you could take my word for it …). Academic writing is not easy and nobody can do it without effort. I have always suspected this, but having talked to some of the most prolific academic writers of our generation, I can confirm that they all spoke about being stuck sometimes. The difference between them and us is that they don't stay stuck. They have strategies for moving projects on, which they deploy immediately and effectively. In this section, I will set out some of the many ways we can get help with our (not) writing.

TALK ABOUT WRITING

Here, I do not mean bothering innocent bystanders with the problem you are having explaining the relevance of your theoretical framework (for this kind of affliction, please Section 1, Writing out loud). I mean finding people that you can be honest with about your actual writing process and progress. In an ideal world, we would all share our writing realities with our colleagues, but I am well aware that the ambiance in many academic departments is far from ideal. Not talking about our writing, not sharing honestly with each other hurts everyone. We have all grown so silent on what we enjoy and don't enjoy, which parts of our papers we find easy, boring and infuriatingly difficult, that those of us who struggle to write take this silence to mean that we are the only ones who find it hard. If we don't share our failures and laugh at our rejections, then we each have to learn all the lessons ourselves. This makes our learning slow and reduces our resilience. It means we can never benefit from the hard-won experience of others. We can neither give nor receive advice and support. It also means we can never have the serendipity of stumbling across a colleague who is a genius in exactly the part of the process that we hate most.

I have presented bits of the book you are reading to various groups throughout my academic career. I have talked about how hard it is for me to write and some of the things that help me move through that in public since I was a post-doc. I have never ever presented this material in a room full of academics who looked at me as if they had no idea what I was talking about. I have always been met with recognition and relief. And people willingly added their stories and their writing tics and tips long before I started to interview people formally for this book. But it is like breaking a taboo. Opening up a space to talk about our writing processes one to one or in a group setting is something every academic writer can benefit from, whether they love to write and skip to their keyboard each morning or haul themselves into their office and open their files with a sense of dread.

If your immediate academic setting is not a safe one to discuss your writing realities in, then you will find plenty of virtual groups online where you can be honest, ask questions openly and get support and advice from generous souls in other places. Do some research and see if you can find yourself a safe, supportive and vibrant community of people ready to cheer you up and cheer you on.

Letting someone else into your struggle to write can be difficult, but it opens the door for such a raft of support and new behaviours that it is always worth doing. For far too many of us, seeking out any kind of support is seen as a last resort. The truth is that the more people you write with, the more you learn about writing and yourself as a writer. Better still, if you can let others help you with your writing, you will not only learn more, but also learn faster. There are lots of ways to do this and here are just some of the possibilities.

GET A CHEERLEADER

Sometimes we need guidance. Sometimes we need advice. Sometimes we need the red pen of an editor to help. Sometimes we just need the pom poms. All we need is moral support. Someone who sees us. Someone to tell us we are doing great: Wow. Seven words. Man, that is great. We don't need intervention in our process or suggestions on our content, just a cheerleader. Until we learn to be our own cheerleader.

GET A RUBBER DUCK

I know of a ground-breaking software engineering department where they have a rubber duck. The duck sits around on the tops of filing cabinets or the ends of shelves minding his or her own business until someone gets stuck with a bit of code. The stuck person takes the duck to a colleague and asks them to hold it while they explain the problem that they are stuck with, asking, 'will you be my rubber duck?'. The colleague takes the duck and holds it and listens closely to the description of the problem. The duck is a reminder that they need to not make suggestions, ask questions or interfere with the stuck colleague's narrative of their problem. They are just being asked to listen closely and encourage the speaker with their attention and body language. It never takes long for folks to get unstuck and the duck goes back on the shelf to wait for its next opportunity to help.

The rubber duck is genius because it is a shared cultural symbol in that group that everyone gets stuck, that being stuck is not a serious or permanent problem, that all you need to do is to share your problem with someone (anyone) who will give you their attention and be rooting for you to overcome it, that you are the one who has the power to get unstuck and that we all need to take turns being stuck and helping others get unstuck in the marvellous party game that is academic life.

GET A WRITING BUDDY

I don't mean some line manager figure who sees this role as a way of checking up on you, or a smart arse who writes effortlessly and leaves you feeling like you just don't have all the pieces of the puzzle. I mean someone else who is struggling to write and understands your experiences but does not judge you. You need to find someone you can be honest and open with. Meet up and have a great big moan. Laugh and cry and make fists at the writing and the NOTwriting together. Then take a joint deep breath and make a promise to write a tiny thing: some headings; a paragraph; a list of papers you'll need to read. Then meet again in a week. Compare notes. Celebrate, commiserate, rinse and repeat. This is really about accountability, not feedback. This can get tricky if one member of the pair gets unstuck and the other doesn't. You need to persevere with each other as well as with the writing. Meeting weekly is really helpful because it brings pace to our writing (or reflections on notwriting). It is also important to set the meeting times out in advance and not have them depend on producing something or they will peter out and the accountability will be lost. Keep the faith and help each other step out of judgement and into tentative writing habits.

GET A WRITING MENTOR

All of us find our own angst endlessly interesting. For some folks, finding out that others have the same doubts and challenges is liberating and an instant salve. For others, it just looks like more angst that they can't deal with. So, if the idea of seeking out someone in the same position as you makes you feel like putting your head on the table, then maybe you could try to find a mentor instead. A mentor is someone who may have struggled in the past and can be empathetic towards your situation, but who is not struggling right now (or at least does not need to share their struggle with you). A writing mentor is someone who can do this specifically for your writing. They are someone who can talk through lots of the ways forward suggested in this book, help you to decide on a strategy and then meet with you to help you reflect on whether that strategy is working and how you can change or adapt your practices to get writing. They don't have to be more senior than you (in dog years, citations or position in the university), they just have to have been there and got themselves back. It needs to be someone you trust who will also trust you.

GET A WRITING MENTEE

In fact, one of the signs that I am notwriting is that I am very motivated to help others with their notwriting! What started as a distraction and a form of virtuous avoidance for me has turned into my best therapy. One of the most amazing things is that helping other folk get unstuck unsticks me. Maybe it reminds me that I always find a way out of the stuck. Maybe it allows me to rehearse my repertoire of ways of getting unstuck. Maybe I am speaking mostly to myself. Anyway, it works! I love helping others get unstuck! It leads to smiling, internal skipping in the workplace and actual dancing in my kitchen. And writing. My own writing. Sometimes I think that as long as there is flow, it doesn't matter whose actual flow it is. Experiencing it leads to more. But that leads to an interesting thought: you might be exactly the writing coach that somebody else needs! Even if you get stuck a lot. Especially because you get stuck a lot. Even while you are stucker than a stuck thing right now. I'll leave that with you …

GET AN EDITOR

Sometimes, when you know you need to improve a draft but you don't know *how*, and/or all the support and cheering of peers is lovely but doesn't help you address the need to uplevel your work, what you need is someone experienced and kind to get their red pen out and take the role of editor. An editor is someone who gives you very specific feedback on a particular piece of work. They will actually write on your draft, changing wording, reordering arguments and identifying the bits that are missing and/or surplus to requirements. This is a really valuable contribution, and it can change your writing not just for the one piece that they have taken the time to mark up for you, but for all your future writing if you let it. The experience of having our own work pulled up by its bootstraps by someone practised in writing for the top journals in your field can be a career-changing one. I know it was for me. Suddenly, the *how* is laid bare and the norms of your field become both transparent and accessible to you. It can be a great unlocking.

A lot of experienced writers are practised at editing other folks' work and will be happy to spend a couple of hours scribbling on your current draft without any thought of taking any kind of credit. It is nice to add an acknowledgement at the end of your paper to thank them for their comments on an earlier draft, if the journal allows, once you get through the review process. Some people will be glad to help by editing your work and will ask you to add them as an author. This can work out well for both parties and if the work they do genuinely improves the work then that might be appropriate. Resist any arguments to have their name go first on your paper, though: this is not a generous soul with your best interests at heart. Look for someone else to help you.

You could also have a look at Section 4 if someone generous enough to do this for you doesn't immediately spring to mind.

JOIN A WRITING GROUP

Since writing is hard and we all need to get constructive feedback to progress, writing groups can help you because they set a pace (weekly or monthly check-ins, for example) and also have you make a commitment to another human being. In particular, if you are feeling the slide towards notwritingatall, this kind of public commitment coupled with empathetic peers and gentle feedback can really help. Some writing groups read each others' work and give feedback on the actual writing, and some just comment on the writing progress. In my experience, both kinds of feedback are amazing and necessary for gaining perspective and tackling 'the next draft', but if you are stuck then considerations of how to improve your writing feel quite far away and also can feel a bit threatening. Or pointless. If you are notwriting something then really discussing how to make the seven words you glared at for the whole of last month a wee bit better isn't that helpful at this point. If this is where you are standing, then a group that concentrates on progress (seven words, wow, Seonaidh, you have, like, doubled your output this month, that's epic) is probably more what you need right now.

There is a lot written about writing groups in the academic literature and I've noticed that they often seem to make the assumption that writing groups are for beginners or doctoral students. Pay no attention: everyone can benefit from writing groups.

If a whole group feels too hard, try asking just one person you trust to intervene with you and help you to make a small, quiet start. In an ideal world this might be your PhD supervisor or a senior academic in your own institution that you could meet informally (see Get a writing mentor in this section). I know, though, that the experienced writers and the folk who might look from the outside like they have 'mentor' written all over them (all the publications, all the status, all the years of experience, etc.) might not be the best people to ask. I have found that people with writing skills do not always have the mentoring skills necessary to nurture the writing skills in others. Writing well is hard, and not everyone is happy to show you their own struggles.

GET A CO-AUTHOR

A co-author is someone who shares the writing of a paper or book with you. Many of the scholars I interviewed spoke about how writing a single-author paper was materially different from writing with a co-author. Not just that it took much longer (although they did say that), and longer in a way that seemed hard to believe or justify (and they said that, too), or that it was much harder to write (which they also discussed), but that it was a completely different process. And crucially perhaps for us, they all noted that it was much harder to find momentum: more difficult to make it come to the top of the 'to do' list; tougher to commit time to it; and that they could measure the fallow periods of a single-author paper in years. Some of them spoke about the single-author process with dread, some with wistfulness, but they all understood it as different from writing with others in ways that were concrete and significant. I often use the analogy of a marathon for writing over the course of a career, a book or a thesis. This is true in all the positive ideas that it conjures (lower running speed, over longer distances and times) but it is also true in some more negative ways (lonely, gruelling, pushing to or past your personal limits). A marathon is like writing single-author pieces; writing with others (when it works well) is more like running a relay race. Yes, there is sprinting, but there is also a plan to hand it on to someone else at the end of your sprint. The same distance can be covered with less time and less individual cost. If you know in your heart that you will never learn to pace yourself and are a sprinter by nature, better get yourself a relay team.

If you are prone to getting stuck then, a co-author can be a magical thing. This is a person with a vested interest in you, in your work and in getting you unstuck. You don't need to worry about calling them up to discuss being stuck with a section of the writing because your stuck is their stuck. They can qualify as a built-in rubber duck/writing buddy/accountability partner and maybe even a mentor. You can't automatically assume everyone will relish having these roles. Some folks would prefer it if you just go away and write 'your bit' and not bother them. However, finding a co-author with whom you can be open and honest about your process can be seriously liberating for folks like me whose writing process isn't always a straightforward one.

If you are smart, you will seek out a co-author with different skills to you. We all talk about 'writing' as if it is one thing. A single process. In fact, it is a wild collection of different skills (see Section 3, Writing is a single skill). At the macro level it includes: big picture thinking and attention to detail; communicating brand new ideas and structuring them carefully; and summarising the status quo and challenging it. At the micro level it is: building and weaving; summarising; reading critically; drawing graphs and diagrams; formatting references; structuring arguments; framing arguments; explaining ideas; and convincing readers (convincing reviewers!). These are all really different tasks, suited to people with different outlooks, skills and temperaments. The truth is that we are all good at different parts of what we call 'writing' and rubbish at others. One colleague told me she always gets stuck with the introduction of her papers. It made me wonder how many of us always get stuck at the same part of the process or at the same point in a paper? The glorious thing is that although each of us might get stuck in the same section, process or stage, this stuck place is different for different people. I draw a mean diagram, but I haven't written an abstract in 20 years. If you hate to write literature reviews then find someone who loves them. If you can't ever get the graphs right then find someone who lives to perfect them. If you find the data collection is a grind then look for someone who can think of nothing better. This way you will travel faster and also more lightly through your academic writing. This is writing not as a relay race, but as a curling match: some folks throw whilst other folks sweep, everyone aiming at the same target but with very different actions.

If you are wise, though, you will look for people you like. I have co-authored with around 50 different scholars over the years, from a wide range of disciplines and at all different levels of the academic ladder. Some people I have co-authored with across many papers for many years. But they all have something in common: they are wonderful human beings. Of course, I have found myself in the writing equivalent of marriages of convenience once or twice, but on the whole I have chosen my co-authors because they are lovely and because I would really like to write with them. My longest-standing, most prolific collaboration is a perfect example of this. We both started our first lectureship in the same department on the same day. By the end of our induction course we had established that we shared a sense of humour, a passion for qualitative data and a wish to write with someone in the same physical locale. We met in her office and set out our different skills and knowledge. We decided to see what would happen if we took her discipline into my field, and my discipline into her field. We wrote a conference paper on one idea and the tiniest grant proposal imaginable on the other. And 25 years later we are still writing together. We can finish each other's sentences, remotely, over video calls, without seeing the other person's screen. Honestly, without her, my academic career would have been entirely different. Her accountability alone has had me write more and better than I ever would have left to my own devices. She has been a co-author on nearly half of the things I have written.

FORM A WRITING TEAM

I have been lucky, for sure; but it's not just me. Most of the established scholars that I spoke to identified these kind of long-term writing relationships that had spanned their careers. Writing teams can speed up your writing and reduce the burden on any one person per paper for sure, but they can also increase the quality of the output because of the built-in discussion and review processes that they entail. Being able to pass on a draft to someone else can also provide an excellent way to get the paper (rather than the writer) unstuck! People who write in teams describe them as an ongoing conversation, often sustained by friendship and always driven by shared curiosity that is punctuated by outputs along the way. In fact, when they described how they 'write' together it amazed me how much of their process wasn't based on writing at all, but centred on talking. This, I think, is the key to their speed and high-quality output.

Writing in teams brings the very best and worst experiences of academic writing. Lots of people have tales to tell of co-authors who took credit for other people's hard work. Interestingly, though, my data suggest that even folks who have been seriously let down or badly treated by co-authors in the past still prefer to write with others than write on their own. It is about finding the right writing partners. If you do work in teams you need to learn to deploy the skills of agreeing specific roles and making expectations clear to everyone at the outset.

At the stage of agreeing a storyboard for the paper (see Section 1, Storyboards) with my co-authors we often also agree author order. The person with the most, or most significant, bits to write will lead the paper and become the first author. It can all change over time, of course, but it is useful to set out a detailed intention for the paper that can be discussed and agreed on. Whoever agrees to lead the paper will drive it forward and incorporate the contributions made by the whole team, thereby earning that first-author position! Otherwise, joint ownership can segue into low ownership or even no ownership, and we all know what happens to those papers.

Writing teams can be strategic. The United Kingdom (UK) Research Excellence Framework[1] initially wouldn't allow co-authors from the same department to both count any jointly published outputs, so a lot of UK writing teams from my generation are geographically dispersed. I know of a group of scholars who vary the first author of their joint papers depending on who is up for promotion. Most writing teams rotate the first-author role on the basis of turn taking, each one championing a different paper and driving it forward. In the time that a single scholar can write one paper, a team of three can write three, each contributing to every paper but only taking the lead on one. These kinds of arrangements can only take place within relationships where there is a great deal of trust, reciprocity and a long-term view. If you can build a team like this, it could certainly change your career. But they don't start from ambition, they start from a bond between colleagues or friends.

GO ON A WRITING COURSE

So few of us were explicitly taught to write (McGrail, Rickard & Jones, 2006). Most of us learned implicitly through a mixture of reading academic literature and having our own work critiqued first by supervisors and then by mentors, co-authors and reviewers (see Section 4, Improving your writing). Why is it that we are supposed to learn the hardest things in life, like writing and parenting, by osmosis? If you haven't got a spare decade available for this 'self-directed apprenticeship' model, then you might consider signing up for a course. This can point you towards the basics, help you see how academic writing is judged and, if you are lucky, give you a circle of peers that morphs into a writing group over time. At the very least you might undo (or even just learn the name of) one of your bad habits and find other humans who are ready to be honest with you about writing habits (yours and theirs). As more and more of us are 'encouraged' to write more and more, more and more courses about academic writing are being designed and run to address the gap between [sees academic paper] and [writes academic paper]. That can only be a good thing. A good place to start is by looking at the organisations of academics (that used to be called learned societies) for your region or discipline to see whether they offer anything interesting. Your own (or a neighbouring) institution might run something relevant. Try searching online if there is nothing geographically feasible. Even if it is offered as part of training for doctoral or early-career colleagues and you have not technically fit this description since before some of those folks were born, don't rule it out. Celebrate the fact that the next generation is being better prepared and join right in. If you feel conspicuous, take a friend. Also don't discount more general classes on writing non-fiction. You'll be surprised how relevant the advice is, especially if you have a book in your mind's eye. If you can't find a writing course, you can bet you are not the only one looking for this kind of advice, so find an expert and host one!

TRY CO-WRITING

If you are writing a sole-author piece, or you don't have any official collaborators with whom you can be open about your writing process, or you know other folk in your circle that are stuck but they are working in different disciplines, you might want to give co-writing a try. This is where two or more people sit down at an agreed time and write for an agreed length of time, or in an agreed pattern but on different projects. I have done this with good friends over the internet (even in different time zones!), I have joined in with complete strangers from an online writing forum and I have set up departmental co-writing events for interested colleagues and even whole doctoral programmes.

At the informal end of the spectrum this looks like two friends prearranging a time where they show up in person or online and write for a short time on whatever they are stuck with. I have done this daily for a week or so with a friend who had got very stuck and I was way too far away for hugs and too stuck myself to be of much help. We agreed to meet at the same time every day online. We started with a 20 minute session, then built up to half an hour and by the end of the week we were writing together (on our own, unrelated projects) for an hour each day. Before we started to write we told each other what we were going to work on and at the end of our writing session we gave a wee progress update and then described the next step. The writing times themselves were silent. This process is always really productive for me, although I realise that it is some people's idea of a nightmare. If, in the words of my dear friend, you just need to 'sit on your ass and stop getting up to go to the fridge', it is definitely worth a try. See Section 6 for examples of online co-working communities.

An even more civilised version of this is where you show up together at your favourite coffee shop and write in companionable silence with a delicious beverage to hand. Note that the main difference here from the other kinds of support is that your co-writer(s) is (are) simply witnessing your writing, they are not intervening in it or giving you their opinion of it in any other way apart from approving your showing up and moving your hands across the page or keyboard, as they show up and do the same.

I have also set this up more formally, with colleagues. I booked the nicest meeting room on campus and set it up with lots of lovely big desks and extension cables so that we could plug a laptop in at each one. I invited anyone in the department who might like to come. About 12 of us signed up. We had lunch together and each of us said a few words about what we were writing. Then we went to sit down in the booked room and write. We wrote in silence for an hour, each at a different table, with mobiles switched off and no internet access. Once the hour was up we had a break for tea and coffee. I brought cake and biscuits to share. We went back to our room to write and wrote for another hour. Afterwards, we each said a few words about what we had written and when we were next planning to work on it. Some colleagues worked on recalcitrant PhD chapters, others on drafts of papers. One turned notes from reading into paragraphs of a literature review. Someone else handwrote a whole outline. The time flew by and nobody got stuck. Together we wrote thousands of words! At least one of us had a wee cry and another told me afterwards he had had an epiphany. Just from the discipline and companionship of sitting down together to write. I know of doctoral programmes that also use this model and have had great feedback from participants.

Co-writing works because it filters out all the external disruptions from people dropping by or emails pinging into your inbox, as well as the natural interruptions of writing itself. Instead of coming to a place in our writing where we need a piece of evidence to back up our argument and spending half an hour trawling through bibliographic databases for the right piece or digging in boxes for half-remembered papers we definitely put somewhere safe, we can simply type '(add ref)' and keep going. Not only does this maintain your train of thought and writing momentum, but it also gives us a 'to do' list for those times when we are very uninspired indeed, or only have a short time between meetings (see Section 1, Take a note).

PAY FOR STRUCTURED SUPPORT

There are all kinds of help out there to get folk writing. Once you start looking you will see that help is everywhere. Take a second to ask yourself why that is: it is because (a) writing can be hard and (b) we all get stuck. You, my friend, are not a freak of nature. Stuck is normal. There is a whole industry out there ready to help you with that! There are services which you can pay to help you make deadlines and check up on you. There are programmes where you work with a coach or go through steps to get writing. There are a load of books on writing! There are free groups where you can find writing buddies or sign up to post your daily word count. There are online communities who feel your pain and can help you feel like you are not alone (trust me, you are not alone). Check out Section 6 for some ideas.

One thing that applies to all these sources of support: although digital connections are great, and can work particularly well once relationships have become established, or when face-to-face meetings are just not possible, in-person support is always more beneficial. This is reported when people speak about co-authors, writing groups, buddies, co-writing, mentors or writing teams. I don't know what it is about the molecules of two or more human beings jiggling in the same room, that it makes ideas flow, confidence levels rise, problems unknot, arguments clarify and words emerge with less effort. You'd have to ask the scientists about that. Although you should never dismiss digital facsimiles of shared human experience when you are stuck, if you can wrangle meetings where people sit down and talk together, then you will find that is always better.

LAST WORD

Writing is hard. Asking for help is hard. I know it feels like asking for help about your writing should be doubly difficult. But it isn't. Firstly, because writing is hard, and because talking about writing makes it easier; when you talk to someone else about your writing there's a good chance that you will inadvertently make their writing easier too. Secondly, because we are only going to ask the lovely people for help, remember? But mostly because asking for help is much easier than pretending you don't need any, and much, much easier than being stuck. People might say no. And that can feel frightening, but it probably has nothing to do with you or your writing and everything to do with how their day/week/semester/career/life is going right now. Research shows that asking for help is the top trust-building behaviour between colleagues (Brown, 2018). So, even if they say no, you'll have shifted your relationship with them and they are more likely to think well of you because you are someone who can ask for help. And if you still believe that showing this kind of vulnerability is weakness and therefore to be despised, then check out Brené Brown's work in Section 6 for a masterclass on why that is simply not true.

Ask somebody for help. If you don't know them very well, then probably don't ask them to be your lifelong mentor the first time you meet them in the corridor. Ask if they've got half an hour for a coffee to discuss a specific section of a paper you are working on. You don't even need to tell them you are stuck. Go on: do it by email if that feels easier (and easier for them to say no). And if they say no, don't make up 3 million stories about how they obviously think you are rubbish, just tell yourself they are busy and ask somebody else. If there's no one in your immediate vicinity, ask folks at conferences or in online groups. Or pay for some support. But do ask for help.

Everyone gets stuck

Everyone works on multiple writing projects

Everyone has a best time of day to write

Everyone writes rubbish first drafts

Everyone finishes more projects faster when they write with others

Everyone gets rejected all the time

Writing is more than one skill. **Everyone** is better at some writing skills than others

NOTE

1.   See Glossary entry on Research Excellence Framework.

3.   Shift your thinking

At the start of this book I noted that the things that can help us get unstuck with our academic writing fall into three main camps: trying new things; getting support; and shifting your thinking. The previous two sections centred mostly on the first two of these: a wide range of new things to experiment with; and the ways in which others can help us. This section will concentrate on the third piece of the puzzle: how we can change the ways we think about ourselves as writers, our writing practices and the things we write. It is a bunch of ways in which we can reframe this whole writing thing for ourselves. If you have tried getting others involved in your writing processes and you have had a go at several of the practical strategies for getting unstuck and these have had no traction on your writing, then it could be that you need to reframe. Have a look in some of these circus mirrors on the next few pages to see whether any of them seem familiar to you and/or need to be shifted out of your tent.

WRITING IS A SINGLE SKILL

In Section 2, Get a co-author, I raised the idea that writing isn't a single task but is a process that involves the bringing together of lots of different skills in an iterative and often collaborative way to make a single output. This is why writing single-author pieces is so very hard and takes inordinately more time than writing with others. And I don't mean in a linear, additive way: as if working with one co-author will reduce the amount of time it takes to write a paper by a third; then working with two co-authors will reduce the amount of time by two-thirds ($t = p-n/3$, where p is the energy required to produce the paper and n is the number of co-authors). Not having co-authors somehow has a multiplicative effect on writing timescales ($t - p(p^n)$), where n is the number of co-authors you should've had!). In our time-poor experience of academic writing, this may be part of the reason that single-author papers are getting less and less common (see for example Henriksen, 2016 for an account of this across the social sciences, and Tietze, Glam & Hofmann [2020] for the news that less than 3% of physics papers are single authored). Besides, who wants to collaborate with themselves?!

The interviews I conducted revealed seven distinct skill sets that make up what we rashly refer to as 'writing'.

Reading

The reading starts with searches to find all the stuff you need. For me, this looks like a combination of raking through my files and favourite bibliographic databases (of course I have favourites!) to find the most relevant things. As I read, I will search forward (through citations) and backwards (through the references) of the most central pieces until I feel like I have found all the main building blocks that I am going to need. I take handwritten notes as I read. I note anything interesting in the specific paper but also any agreements or disagreements with other studies. In my notes, I use an asterisk in a circle to signal to myself that I need to include a specific point when I come to writing or follow something up later. I keep reading until I have stopped seeing new references and begin to feel that I have a feel for the field. When I am ready to draft, I will not refer to the papers themselves, but to my notes.

Reading doesn't always happen first, or in one lump, especially for qualitative researchers. I find reading a slow and arduous task, not least because I generally read FAR too much before I begin to draft. Although I can write in tiny slices of time and never lose my train of thought, I do tend to binge read, immersing myself for days in the literature until I feel I have it all in my head. I do take notes on each piece I read as I go, but my notes are not good enough to stand the test of time, so I need to move to drafting quite quickly or I will often have to reread things from scratch. I don't retain the detail of what I have read for any length of time, to the extent that in the days when I was wading my way through a pile of physical papers, I would put a green sticker on the ones I had read in an effort to keep track of what I had already seen.

First Draft

One of the most interesting things to come out of my interviews was the idea that writing a first draft is a materially different skill than any other kind of writing. Some people hate it and some people love it, but they all agreed that it was a different experience to write a first draft of something than working on all the drafts that followed. The first draft can certainly be the slowest. It is definitely the biggest writing task of all, in terms of pages, words, time and energy. Big. But if you are able to treat it lightly and think of it as inherently scruffy and imperfect, it can also be the fastest kind of writing. All of the ideas, quotes and problems spill out on to the page without judgement or censure. For me, I approach this like a jigsaw. I write lots of jigsaw pieces and worry about how to put them together another day. They definitely all (or at least mostly) belong in the same box, even if I am not completely sure what the exact picture on the box is going to be. I see my jigsaw as part of the big jigsaw that is the stuff already written. A meta jigsaw, if you like. Matryoshka jigsaws, maybe.

There will always be pieces you find boring to write (the sky of academic papers) and bits you long to focus on, but you have to write something for every piece and lay them all out. Like the jigsaw, once I have written all my 'pieces' and laid them out, I am ready to start. My first draft process ends with me reordering and grouping and ungrouping and regrouping my paragraph pieces until I have a rough line of argument.

Framing

This is the process of demonstrating how your jigsaw fits with the big jigsaw of everything else that is already written and how it adds value, changes things, shifts perspective and/or extends or downright challenges what has gone before. People sometimes refer to this as 'positioning', which is another great implicit metaphor that makes me think of orienting your piece on a map of the written world (this is a sort of south-west-facing paper of mid-range altitude with dense forests, backing on to the previously well explored grasslands of recycling instructions. It provides both a novel perspective of the grasslands and some insight into the forests themselves). It is what reviewers like to call defining the paper's 'contribution'. This is difficult work (see Section 6 for help) because it means you have to have a pretty good grasp of what went before plus a big-picture view of your own piece. One of these is gained through a great deal of reading, whilst the other is gained through the practice of standing back and asking 'so what' about your own work. However, done well, strong framing elevates a paper from descriptive (reporting findings) to insightful (joining the debate). Some people frame using specific theories. Some folks use previous arguments or norms in the field as their point of departure. Framing might not contribute many pages to a piece but it is the most important and potent element of academic writing. Some people are really good at this. Some senior researchers reported that this is the bit they contribute to nearly every paper they write now. A lifetime of reading and reviewing leaves them well placed to do this kind of work and it can be hard to achieve at the start of your career. (I seriously impact my ability to do it well by insisting on setting nearly every paper I write in a different literature. Not clever. Add this to your list of things not to do, please.) Don't be afraid to ask people to help you with the standing back. It is always easier to see why someone else's ideas are important and, when we are writing, the very detail orientation that we need for editing and polishing can make our heads far too full to frame effectively.

Editing

This is the business of working through a draft of a paper and making changes, insertions and deletions and identifying missing puzzle pieces that would make it a better next draft. One of the key editing tasks is to make sure that a line of argument runs through the whole paper. But honestly, editing can involve everything from spotting typos[1] and ironing out clunky phrases to completely restructuring the previous draft and/or writing completely new sections. When you have several authors, one of the editing roles is to try to shift the piece from being a collection of bits to something that has a single voice. Overall, it is a focus on 'how' the paper is doing the work of presenting evidence and joining ongoing debates.

Some of the experienced writers I spoke with loved to take the work of others and edit it into something more coherent and effective. They saw it as a way of adding value to a paper more efficiently than they could if they were starting writing from scratch. A couple of folks explicitly mentioned editing as a means of upskilling early-career researchers. This is one of the reasons that I mention finding a friendly editor in Section 2, Get an editor. If you excel at this stage of the writing and don't enjoy the process of writing the first draft, you might need to seek out a first-draft writer to feed you material to shape.

Editing is also iterative. Don't expect to do it just once. One of the most experienced writers I spoke to recalled a paper which hit version 64 before it was submitted to a journal, although he did admit that some of those edits were relatively minor. Another estimated an average of 10 full, distinct drafts before her writing was ready to be shared with anyone outside her writing team.

Summarising

This is the dark art of saying the same thing, but much smaller. It is the skill you need to be able to write effective abstracts. It is very tempting (and very common!) to reiterate bits of your introduction and call that an abstract. Although this will likely set out the context of your problem it will not really summarise your paper. I can't tell you how many grant applications I have read that spend 200 of their precious 250 abstract word budget telling me the most general of things (which in my field is that climate change is happening, or that the United Nations have 17 Sustainable Development Goals), setting out the macro context of their problem and including just a single line saying what they will focus on, without ever mentioning what they will actually *do*. Some journals have structured abstracts which are designed to trick you into avoiding this very human approach. They ask you to say a sentence or two under a range of specified headings. One journal I produced a structured abstract for, for example, asked for a total of 250 words which included explanations of:

1. purpose;
2. design/methodology/approach;
3. findings;
4. originality (sometimes called contribution);
5. limitations; and
6. implications.

This can be really helpful and, if you are not used to writing abstracts, I suggest finding a journal in your field with structured abstracts, copying the headings they advocate, filling in the blanks and then deleting the headings. Hey presto: a perfectly formed abstract which gives as much weight to the method, findings and significance of your paper as it does to the context and problem.

Summarising is also an important, but less explicit, part of writing an introduction (what will be in the paper) and a conclusion (what has been said so far). It really is worth cultivating this skill as it will stand you in good stead for everything, from writing your bio to making great presentations. The most radical form of summarising is crafting your title. This is the extreme sports version of summarising. Your whole thesis in nine words. Strangely, I love witing titles and hate writing abstracts in equal measure.

Polishing

This is the process of taking an edited draft and raising the rigour, language and referencing quality to give the piece the best possible outcome. This includes targeting a specific journal, or rank of journal. So, for example, tying arguments into specific debates in the journal you have your heart set on, or making changes to a piece to make it suitable for a 4* journal[2] in your field. It involves a lot of tweaking and feedback from a wide range of peers through conferences or friendship circles to widen your perspective of your paper and help you see how to make it clearer and stronger. Closing loopholes, deleting hostages to fortune, killing your darlings (see Section 1, Take a note) and, often, conforming to mainstream (or specific journal) norms. This stage is not always included. In fact, some authors rolled their eyes at this kind of work, acknowledging that it took a very long time and many drafts beyond their interest in the paper, so they preferred to not do it and forego the possible advantages of a slightly better journal.

Finishing

This is about all the final details. It is formatting your headings to match the submission requirements of your target journal, or your university's thesis style guidelines. It is checking you have all the references that you cited in your reference list and that they are in the right order and the correct format. It is making sure that your heading numbers are consecutive. It is changing the whole document into UK English if you have written in US English and vice versa, depending on where you are sitting and where the journal you are submitting to is sitting. It is tidying up tables and checking the legends on your graphs. I always think that this will take a couple of hours and it always takes me a couple of days. If you have time to do this (aka if you leave yourself enough time to do this), it is quite a pleasing task. Done at high speed, in the middle of the night with the deadline fast approaching (for example!), it is singularly stressful. However, it is necessary work, not least because while if it is done well it will be completely invisible to the reader, if it is done half heartedly then it will jar the eye of the reader and set off the 'shoddy work' siren in someone's head. We have all spent years of reading finished manuscripts, many of us regularly correct student work and most of us have developed a psychopathic tendency to spot errors. Come on, tell me you've never rolled your eyes at a grocer's apostrophe in a menu or on a shop sign? (No? Really? Just me then!) Academics are trained to spot this stuff. A lifetime of wielding a red pen makes us finicky readers. That is who you are dealing with – a mirror image of your own picky grammar police but with the added bonus of not giving you the benefit of the doubt; pedants without sympathy.

Personally, I leave my finishing to the end, unless I am really struggling to get started, and then I use finishing tasks like finding and formatting references or fiddling with an individual clunky sentence as a way to break into my writing process and get started again. Keep a 'to do' list of teeny finishing tasks to hand in case you need them for giving you a sense of progress on a busy meeting day, or want them for the days when five minutes on the timer feels like an eternity.

The idea that writing is actually seven different skill sets raises some interesting questions. First of all, noticing the different tasks involved in 'writing' allows us to separate them out and do one at a time. I know this sounds really obvious, but you'd be amazed how many of us are layering up two or three (or seven!) of these very different processes, all pretty tricky in their own right, and trying to do them at the same time. And I've found that a lot of folk who layer these processes up (a) can find themselves stuck and (b) find it hard to figure out what the source of the stuck is. A lot of folks who are NOTwriting that I've worked with are trying to edit (and also sometimes polish and finish!) while they are drafting. This might be you if you are in the habit of taking a whole afternoon to write a paragraph, only to score it out the next morning. Some people blur their reading and framing to great effect, but for others, this same blurring just leads them to paralysis and despondency as the whole thing gets enormous and unmanageable. If you are doing several of these processes at once, without getting stuck, that's brilliant. But if you are stuck then consider doing one at a time for a while to see if it helps with your progress. A lot of people panic at the idea of doing just one of these things in any given draft because it sounds like it will take much longer to get to a finished piece, but if you are stuck then sometimes separating them out can really speed you up. If I asked you to paint a piece of wood you wouldn't try to undercoat it and top coat it at the same time, brush in each hand. You'd put the different coats on one at a time, building them up layer by layer. The finished piece will look all the better for it.

To separate drafting and editing, start by using the tricks in Section 1 on drafts to concentrate on creating flow and practise not judging the quality of the output. Remember to measure in time, not words (see Section 1, Goals). Using the headings technique is really helpful for me here (see Section 1, Placeholders). Ask your inner editor to step away from the process for now and just type random stuff that needs to be somewhere in your paper in any old order. You can ask her to come back and sort it out for you, once you are ready, but don't allow her to get in the way of the flow of the first draft.

To separate reading and framing, try making notes on just the paper you are reading, focusing on its detail (making pieces for your jigsaw). Once you have a sheaf of notes on a bunch of papers, then stand back and try framing (working out the picture on the box). Notice where there are gaps in the big picture and either write yourself a boundary statement to say why that piece isn't relevant or read some more to find the jigsaw pieces to fill in the space.

The second opportunity that understanding academic writing as seven different processes or tasks can offer us is in sharing them! These seven processes are all quite different, so any one person is unlikely to be equally good at them all. Or find them all equally fascinating. So ask yourself: Which of these do you find easy? Which do you love? Which ones bore you rigid (you'd be surprised how many experienced writers get really bogged down in things they are perfectly capable of but find toweringly dull)? Where do you get stuck? Is it always with the same kind of task? Is there a skill set missing from your toolbox? Who else might have that skill set? Which skills could you offer to a writing team? If you are shrugging at me right now, in a 'dunno' kind of a way, get curious. Think about your writing processes in a critical (see Section 4, Writing before you launch into a stream of insults though) and detached way. Look at the reviews you get. Ask previous co-authors or supervisors what your top (and bottom) writing skills are. Find this stuff out about yourself and then use it to make your writing life easier and more productive.

Please don't run off with the idea that these seven skill sets are deployed in the order that they are described here. Or in any order at all. They are iterative and interdependent. Start somewhere and spiral out from there. Move back and forth between skill sets as a way of getting unstuck. Just because your paper needs to have a beginning, a middle and an end (in roughly that order!) it does not mean that your writing process need to be done in either a logical or a linear order.

On the whole, we are much less likely to get stuck when we are doing the writing activities that we love and find interesting. Paradoxically, my interviews also suggested that we are much less likely to value the skills that we have ourselves. People regularly apologised to me for the things they were good at in the writing process. Several very experienced writers spoke about how many long years of writing it took for them to 'forgive themselves' for or 'accept' these talents. If you have stellar levels of one of these writing skill sets you need to own that, and then you need to tell people. Writers who can articulate their writing skills are much more likely to find co-authors with complementary ones and are therefore correspondingly less likely to ever have to do the bits they hate again (see Section 2, Get a co-author).

WRITING IS LINEAR

When I was first taught to write stories as a child, I was taught that every story has a beginning, a middle and an end. Even when I was an undergraduate and started writing essays this advice was still being offered to us (aka tell them what you are going to tell them; tell them; tell them what you have told them). What I took from this advice (which is not the same as what I was being told) is that stories (essays, academic writing) ought to be written in the order in which they are intended to be read. Which is not only a completely different idea, but also extremely unhelpful for most writers. Now I have already spoken out against the barbaric practice of trying to start writing your paper, book or thesis at the beginning (see Section 1, Starting at the beginning). My best results have always come from writing the introduction last, if I'm honest, although I know this isn't true for everyone. But the other thing that is implied in a lot of places in this book is that writing is iterative. In other words, the experience and process of writing is more:

than:

and maybe sometimes (speaking for myself):

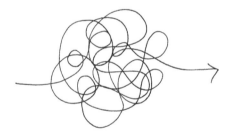

And now you know why the whole thing makes you feel a bit dizzy and some-times nauseous: Try not to take the corners too quickly.

So, have a look at Section 1, Drafts, try starting wherever catches your eye (see also Section 1, Starting at the beginning) and expect to come back to the same bits over and over (and sometimes over and over) again. This won't change the actual writing process, but shifting your expectations can make the iterations seem like a natural part of the writing, rather than an annoying waste of time that you sh/could have avoided if you had done it properly the first time.

ACADEMIC WRITING IS NECESSARY

I am not here to persuade you that you *have* to write. Academic writing can be important (with a small i) in the sense that it is advancing knowledge. As long as you believe that that is still what is happening (Billig, 2013), given how much of it there is now, of course. But (a) if none gets done, few people will be mortally imperilled in the next fortnight and (b) if you don't personally write, no buildings will collapse. Even if your thesis is on concrete. There is a lot written about how important it is to write along the 'publish or perish' lines, but although there is truth in the fact that you may not get promoted as quickly as peers who do all the *same* things as you but write loads, there will be no *actual* perishing. So, here's the thing: Maybe you need to do *different* things. There is more than one way to be an academic. There is more than one way to define success. There is more than one way to get a promotion. There is more than one way to be happy. The system shouts loudly about how publications are the only route, but also quietly promotes great managers, wonderful teachers and ninja administrators. Look around you: there are lots of kinds of work in a university. I'm sure you know at least one happy, successful individual that has bucked the 'publish or perish' trend. No matter what the rhetoric is, no one kind of gift or effort is better than another. Although one might be better suited to you than another (have a look at Section 6 for Michael Bungay Stanier's book *Do More Great Work* if you need some structure to think that through). You might have to learn to go against the prevailing wisdom and listen to yourself and follow your own strengths. Even if you desperately want to be one of the folks who publish, we already know that there is more than one way to contribute to research: generate funding; collect data; supervise students; run conferences. We also know that there is more than one skill set to 'writing' (check out Writing is a single skill in this section). Anyway, I just wanted to come here and say: if you'd like to write, then here I am with my bucketful of tactics and mind shifts that I hope will help you; but if you really wouldn't like to write, then don't.

WRITING IS SERIOUS

All writing. But especially academic writing. Deadly serious. And grown up. And nothing at all to do with emotions. Or maybe only to do with rubbish emotions like fear and frustration and worry.

I had a colleague who asked me to look at some slides for a presentation he was going to deliver to the faculty on research. One word immediately caught my eye: fun. I gave him back the slides with the typos duly checked and the boxes duly lined up and said to him that he had to find another word for 'fun'.

I told him it wasn't professional or appropriate. He declined. He declined because he said that research *should* be fun and work *should* be fun, and if it wasn't fun then why on earth would anyone want to do it? He was right.

It was a bit of a shock to me as a concept at the time. It made me cringe a little bit. Maybe it makes you cringe, too. Passion is fine; playfulness is not. Angst is fine; joy is not. Time to walk past all that nonsense and see if you can find people or processes or questions that make you smile. Also, have a look at Section 1, Doing joyful things now.

WAITING FOR THE MUSE

This is something I subscribed to for a VERY long time. First of all, I told myself that I found it hard to write when I was very busy and stressed because I had too many things running around in my brain in order to be able to find the right headspace to write. This meant, as a beginning academic, that I was more or less writing at weekends and in my annual leave. Less writing being the operative phrase! All that happened was that I never took breaks and I got slower and slower and slower and slower and slower. So I led a life of: at work = busy teaching and doing admin; not at work = not busy therefore should be writing. By telling myself that my muse would not appear while I was busy, I simultaneously ruled out five days of the week, ruined my evenings and weekends and ensured that I would never get a break. See Section 1, Breaks. Perfect recipe for burnout/breakdown/hastening depression (delete as applicable). At the same time I was telling myself that my muse would never come while I was not feeling well. Given the practical fall-out of my 'busy' assumption, I was almost always really tired, my mental health was shot and I had a whole succession of minor illnesses (being constantly run down at the same time as being in contact with 100s of students carrying versions of the common cold from every corner of the world will do that to you). The upshot of these assumptions, working together meant that I perceived myself as perpetually not being able to write, when in fact this was possibly my most effective strategy for turning notwriting into NOTwriting and/or notwritingatall. But is was an attractive strategy in some ways because it meant that it was *not my fault*. See what I did there: created a perfect system for notwriting (and the rest!) whilst simultaneously avoiding any responsibility for that. Genuis.

Then, one day, I saw through the whole thing on a single 11 minute tram journey to work. Let me back up a bit … When I was STUCK as in the episode that opens this book, one of the inexplicable side effects of my NOTwriting my thesis was that I started to write poems. I don't mean that I sat down quietly and decided to try a form of creative writing as an antidote to the stressful situation I was in. The poems arrived fully formed in my head. They woke me up abruptly at 3am, roaring their need to be committed to paper. They did not take 'no' for an answer. They dirled round the inside of my head, like ball bearings in a pinball machine trying to find a way out. As you can imagine, I eventually complied. I got up and I wrote them down on the first thing I could find. In their aftermath I found myself standing in the half dark looking at poetry written in my own handwriting (in green pen once, of all things. Anyone who knows me will vouch for the fact that I would never knowingly write anything in green biro!) feeling like I'd been out walking in a North Isles gale and just a wee bit spooked. Anyway, once I started writing my thesis again, the poems seemed to calm down and stopped coming. They left me curious though. I knew nothing about poetry and so, like any good academic, I embarked on a course about it to see if I could learn to do it 'properly'. I know. I hear you. But I didn't know any better and that is not the point of this story. So anyway, as I was saying, I enrolled on a poetry course at the university where I was lecturing. It had a teacher and a textbook and *homework*. I love homework. And I loved this course. I got on the tram one morning to go into work and remembered with great pleasure that I had my poetry course in the afternoon, right after my last lecture. In my head I rehearsed running out of the lecture theatre, into a sandwich shop equidistant between the class I was giving and the class I was taking and skipping into the room with my lovely poetry people with a moment to spare to eat said sandwich. I took my jotter out of my bag and looked to see what the topic would be and realised with a sinking feeling that I had homework. Homework that I had not done! I quickly looked up the task and found that it was to write a poem. My brain click-clacked through all the appointments and commitments between right now and eating my sandwich in that class and I realised that the only time I had to do it was NOW. Right now, right here on the tram, balancing my bag on my knee, surrounded by commuters on my 11 minute journey to the city centre. Without giving my brain time to go through the whole 'writing needs a muse, muse needs …' malarky, I opened my jotter and wrote a poem. In nine minutes. By the time the tram had pulled up to my stop I had my jotter in my bag and stepped down on to the pavement in the daze of having written an excellent poem. Really good. Probably my best one. As I walked down the hill to my office the whole muse thing was laid bare. I saw that it was just a pair of interconnected and powerful stories I was telling myself. Stories I was hiding behind. And with that they were gone with the whoosh of the tram. Leaving me to face the possibility that if I could write in a rush on a tram on a Tuesday morning when I was exhausted in the middle of a semester then I did not need to wait to not be busy and full of vitality. I could just begin where I was standing right now. A realisation as glorious and freeing as it was terrifying and guilt stricken! It also busted the myth that we need big blocks of time to write.

ENOUGH TIME

One of the most widely believed stories that we tell ourselves about writing is that we need to have, or are waiting for, a big block of time to be able to write. For academics, I wonder whether this idea starts with writing a doctoral thesis[3], which in the UK is a huge, four year study that genuinely does take an hour or two to get back into our heads after a long break so that we can remember where we were up to and begin again.

Perhaps it is because it just takes us such a long time to get into the flow from the cold that we tell ourselves it is hardly worth writing in a two hour block because by the time we get started it is time to stop. Now that might be true the first time we start to write after a long and angst-filled break from writing, but I suspect that for most of us it would not be true if we found a few minutes of flow the first day, so that if we came back to it the next day, the resistance period would be shorter. Resistance is proof of resistance, not of an inability to write, lack of inspiration or being a bad person. The issue here then is not of the amount of time that you perceive that you *have* to write, but the amount of time that you leave between the times you have to write!

A successful entrepreneur I know once pointed out to me a really amazing fact which I think is highly relevant here. There is no such thing as more time. As in: I will write this when I have more time; I would like to finish that paper, but I don't have enough time. You know the one. She told me something that rocked my world: we all have the same amount of time. I'll just let you think about that for a minute. Every person on planet Earth has the same amount of time each day. They just make different decisions on how to allocate that time. If you allocate it to reading social media or learning to play an instrument or playing with your children, you have to pay the opportunity cost of allocating it elsewhere. That's it. And in the same way that if we believe we will save money when we have some left over and find that there is no 'leftover money' there is also no 'leftover time'. If you are genuinely frustrated with your writing output then you should seriously consider allocating it more time. This will mean taking time from something else. I realise that is not easy (and please don't choose time with your children to reallocate!), but it is the bottom line: if you do not allocate time for writing, you will have no writing time. I know. (See Section 1, Goals and Blocks of time and blocking out time for different approaches to this.) Of course, if you have allocated lots of time and you are still not progressing your writing, then this is not your problem and you are almost certainly in a fight with your skill level or your confidence. Have a look at the Where should I start? Flowcharts (pp. 123–129) to see whether any of them are helpful in finding a good starting place for you.

GUILT VERSUS SHAME

So. This is an important distinction that many of us have missed out on. For a lot of my life I thought of these ideas as more or less interchangeable. It wasn't until I read the work of Brené Brown that I understood the difference and why it matters (for your writing as well as for life) (Brown, 2015). She is a shame researcher (I know!) and she defines the difference as:

- Guilt arises from 'I did a bad thing' (behaviour).
- Shame arises from 'I am a bad person' (self).

And it turns out that this is not just semantics. The exact words matter a lot here. Although they feel pretty much the same when you experience shame or guilt, they have different mechanisms. Research shows that guilt happens when we do something that goes against our own values. It is focused on our behaviours. It is a useful warning that poor choices are being made. Reflecting on guilty feelings can motivate us to make a repair and do better next time. Guilt is uncomfortable, but can provoke a healthy response which we can learn from and improve upon. Shame, on the other hand, is something that happens when we feel that we are inherently bad in some way and fear that we may be unlovable and don't deserve to belong to our social groups. Because it is focused on how we perceive ourselves to be and not on specific things we may have done, there is no obvious repair, no built-in motivation for change and no real belief that change is even possible. In short, whilst guilt can change our writing practices (I mean there are other ways, but we are where we are!), shame perpetuates them.

The good news is that even though everyone around you from your supervisor to your parents or your significant other uses shame as a tool, you can step out of this by simply changing your language. So, it is time to change your self-talk from, 'I am a terrible writer' or 'I am lazy and stupid' (just picking a random example from nowhere!) to 'Woah, that paragraph is rubbish' or 'I spent the whole afternoon avoiding the writing I wanted to get done'. Focus on the behaviour and give yourself the chance to grow and change. Remember that we are all good people having bad days or struggling to learn difficult skills. Even months or years of poor decisions about your writing do not make you a bad person. (Have a look at Brown, *Dare to Lead* [2018] in Section 6.)

PERFECTIONISM

Perfectionism is an affliction. It is the disease of believing that if you work hard enough for long enough that you can produce something better and better and if you do enough drafts and are critical enough of yourself and push yourself harder then your work will be perfect. This disease of the mind can so easily become a disease of the body as we drive ourselves into places of exhaustion and a disease of the spirit as we work ourselves into deep despair. It is a mirage. Perfection is not real. It is at best a trick of the eye when looking too long to the horizon in the hot sun. You know dragons, right? Imagine one now. What colour is she? How big? Can you see her clearly in your mind? Yeah. She is not real. Perfection is a dragon. Just because you can picture her clearly, write about her in fables and paint her image across the centuries, it does not mean she exists.

If writing perfection is not real, then why do we pursue it so relentlessly? Human nature is a funny old thing. We pursue perfection exactly because it is unobtainable. Not, as the fervoured perfectionist would have you believe, as a bold act of human envelope pushing. No, it is because seeking perfection makes us safe from ever being done. And if we can never be done, we can never get judged, never have feedback. Then our writing can never be 'bad'. We can stay locked in the 'honour' of the struggle without consequences. Plus, it has the added side benefit of allowing us prove to ourselves that we are rubbish and/or our writing is rubbish. Unfortunately, the human psyche drives us towards certainty, and a bad certainty (this writing is rubbish) is better than the possibility of a good uncertainty (this writing *might* be OK if I keep going and do some more drafts). Uncertainty is terrifying. Therefore, perfectionism is perfect because, as it is not attainable, doom is guaranteed. If this is you (and I know it was me) try to look underneath the striving for perfection to see whether there might be a fear of being judged or a comfort in being mean to yourself underneath.

It took me a lot of years to understand that perfectionism wasn't a strength. If you had interviewed me in the 1990s I would have offered it as a badge of honour. It is a hard habit to break, but it is one of the commonest ways of stopping yourself writing before you begin. Maybe because we make ourselves believe that if it can never be perfect, then there is no point in starting. It is also an excellent strategy for keeping us frozen at the start of a project, spending time on the same activities over and over without actually doing anything scary or dangerous like making progress. If you are someone who starts a paper at the beginning, painstakingly writes a paragraph, scoring out words and phrases over and over until you are happy with it, only to throw the whole lot out the next day and start again, you might be suffering from perfectionism. If you are someone who has written and rewritten your introduction 75 times over the last year and never actually got to the guts of your book chapter, you might want to consider whether you are in search of a dragon (see the misconception that Writing is a single skill in this section). If you are (like me) someone who reads EVERYTHING relevant and then finds an interesting tangent in a neighbouring discipline to add to your reading list, then you could suspect yourself of perfectionism.

I have found two ways to break into this vicious, downwards cycle. The first is my headings trick from Placeholders in this section which entails me starting anywhere. A brilliantly imperfect process to defeat the pursuit of a perfect artefact. It is just a trick, though. The other way is a cure but it is much harder: learn to be kind to yourself. Go boldly. The dragons are just in your head.

NOT FIT TO WRITE

Not every day is a writing day. Some days, when we are hauling ourselves through life and everything is difficult, are not days for writing. If you are only standing up and dressed because you feel like you have no other choice then maybe today is a day to rest rather than force yourself to write. Now, I know that when there are lots of days like this in a row then you begin to feel like if you don't write when you feel low and tired then you will never write. And I deeply understand that there are situations that require more than one day of recovery. But there has to be a balance. So, rest if you can and try to write for 10 minutes if you can't. If in doubt, err on the side of being kind to yourself for a few days and see what happens. If these days go on and on then you need more support than reading a mildly sarcastic book about our crazy writing habits: you need to speak to a human being about getting you and/or your health out of the situation you are in. If you have the slightest suspicion that this may be you, please do that right now. Now. Prioritise it.

WRITING ON PURPOSE

I talked earlier (see Waiting for the muse in this section) about how we can kid ourselves that we have to wait for the muse in order to write. Or the moon to be in the right phase, or a specific table in a single coffee shop to be free. All that. And I pretty much dismissed it out of hand. These things are all just stories we are telling ourselves to shift the responsibility for the notwriting from ourselves to the universe so that we don't have to look at the fact that we are notwriting and deal with it. Looking at the notwriting is hard and dealing with the notwriting is hard, and this is just a very human way of avoiding all the hard things. Fair enough. But sometimes, underneath all of that resistance to knowing and doing the things that will actually help shift us from notwriting to writing, there is something else. A misalignment with what you are trying to do versus your own, deeply held, purpose or values. Your subconscious is holding you back from taking a single further step in what it perceives as the wrong direction for you.

You know the saying, 'those that can, do, those that can't, teach'? I disagree with this wholeheartedly. Teaching is a completely different skill set than doing. Also, it can be far harder. Anyway, there is a thing that can happen in academia that goes more like 'those that can, do, those that are afraid they won't be able to do, become academics'. It is not as catchy, but it can be true. Sometimes people who want to be writers sign up for doctorates because it will lead to a job which means they will get to write for a living, right? Answer: not really! Not unless you find writing PowerPoint presentations just as soul quenching as the novel you have in your mind's eye. Sometimes people who want to create elegant policy or motivating social marketing campaigns lack the self-belief to step up and do it and come to 'hide' in academia. Plenty of managers who dreamed of being captains of industry 'semiretire' into business schools where they think that the pace of life will be less frantic. Spoiler alert: they end up no less stressed or busy but they can't lose anybody's millions and their responsibility for other folks' mortgages diminishes; some do find comfort in that. Let's face it, academia, as a business, is about as low stakes as it comes. In other words, sometimes folk who find themselves cross with their writing are actually at cross-purposes with their purpose. And sometimes this lack of alignment with their purpose slowly erodes their ability to write (and therefore progress in an academic career) over time. They are on a path that is wrong for them and their subconscious is trying to block their advancement any further down that path.

There is a slightly more subtle version of this problem: when writing is out of line with your personal values. When I applied to university in the 1980s I applied for degrees in physics. One university wrote back to me and said that they were closing their physics department, but I could apply for engineering instead. Engineering is just like physics, they said, only applied. Useful. There is a lot of that thinking in universities now. If you ask around in a business school, for example, you will find that practically nobody teaching there has a first degree in business studies. They hail from languages, from psychology and sociology, from engineering as well as the more obviously business-related disciplines such as accountancy and economics. I know biologists who teach entrepreneurship, linguists who teach information management and sociologists who teach marketing. And sometimes that is fine. Walking past your training to teach something that is more useful, practical, in demand. Going where the students flock, where the jobs are. Taking the insights from your base discipline and applying them to an organisational context. Because management is not a discipline, it is an area of application of a whole bunch of other disciplines. But for some people, following market forces and applying their academic thinking to areas which are deemed more lucrative for the university doesn't necessarily fall in line with their values. People who opted to study the natural world in their teens aren't necessarily fulfilled by teaching folk how to run better businesses in their midlife. Whilst teaching and writing might be in line with your purpose, it is possible that the actual material you are teaching and writing could still be out of line with your values. This chasm between what you love and feel passionate about and the things that need to be taught or written is a place in which some people get stuck. If you don't find the thing you are notwriting about FASCINATING then this could be part of the problem for you (see Section 1, Ditching things).

KNOWING WHAT TO DO ISN'T THE SAME AS GETTING UNSTUCK

Here's the thing. If you didn't know me you might think I was a successful writer. If you look at my Google Scholar profile you'll see I have published some well-cited stuff in some pretty fancy journals. But being a successful writer doesn't stop me being a struggling writer. For some of us, stuck is a one-off occurrence. You can learn new approaches or ways of looking at your practices and you will stop being stuck. For me, stuck is my natural home and each project is a new opportunity to be stuck, sometimes in brand new ways. Which is why I have found so many excellent ways to get unstuck and become obsessed with it to the extent that I have written a book about it. Using every trick in the book to get myself writing. Literally.

ENJOYING YOUR WRITING

In the same way that not everyone who writes well writes easily, I have discovered that not everyone who writes likes writing. I am not sure how I feel about academic writing. I definitely love writing more generally. I have always written. Journals, diaries, fiction, poetry. I LOVE writing this book for you right now. But all the papers I have written? I definitely love having written them in the past tense! And it was one of the most satisfying parts of my academic career. But did I enjoy it? I think I was too busy worrying about squandering my privilege as a public servant and at the same time worrying that I wasn't writing enough or writing fast enough to actually like it while it was going on. The ideas I love. The talking I love. The figuring out I love. But the actual writing? I'm not so sure. And I'm not the only one: some of the folks I interviewed for this book did not like writing AT ALL, even though they had written loads. So the good news is that you definitely don't need to like writing in order to be a successful writer. But you might want to have a wee think about that. I'll leave it with you … (see Stanier, *Do More Great Work* in Section 6 for some ways to work through these ideas).

RESISTANCE

Resistance is when we start to feel like the writing might be fighting back. It seems to be actively trying to not get done. Don't take my word for it, ask Stephen Pressfield (2002; see Section 6). I feel it like a force field that seems to hold me at a distance slightly further than arm's length from my keyboard. When it gets into its stride, I find it hard to be in the same room. It is a physical sensation, rather than a cognitive worry loop. This is a sign for me that I have tipped over into NOTwriting and, when that happens, I know I am going to need someone else's help to get out. If you don't have a helpful person to hand, you could try Joli Jensen's strategy of writing about your resistance in what she calls a 'ventilation file', so that you can write out all your fear and loathing for your current writing project and get it off your chest and maybe spark some new perspective on the ideas about you, your writing project or about writing in general that are holding you back (Jensen, 2017, ch. 4).

REGRET

When we stop writing, especially if we have successfully written academic outputs in the past, it is easy to be overcome with a sense of regret and think unkind thoughts about yourself. My PhD was funded by the Science and Engineering Research Council[4] (yes, I'm very old, I know). When my funding came to an end I was mortified that I had not submitted my thesis and full of self-loathing for missing the deadline. As I sat on the floor of my good friend's empty sitting room weeping while she painted the walls a tasteful shade of pink late one night, she listened patiently to my outpouring of grief and shame.

Seonaidh [weeping]:   But it's not finished …
Friend: [paints]
Seonaidh [wailing]:   And I am such an idiot, I can't believe it is so late …
Friend: [paints sympathetically]
Seonaidh [weeping and wailing]:   I always do this. I am rubbish at writing. I hate feeling like this and it's my own fault because I made it late. And now it is late.
Friend: [paints]

[repeat from the top, several times, with feeling]

Friend [points paint brush directly at Seonaidh]:   Look. Nothing you can do can ever change the fact that it is late. It can now never be on

time. You have to accept that and move forward and find a way
to minimise the lateness, but stop wasting your energy lambast-
ing yourself for something that cannot be changed.

Seonaidh [takes sharp intake of breath]:   [paints]

No matter how much you regret not doing any/enough writing yesterday, you cannot change that. You can only change the future. To do that you have to let go of your feelings about NOTwriting previously, draw a line and walk forward. I'm not saying it is easy. Not everyone has a friend with exactly the right balance of empathy and pointed pink paint brush wielding to help them at a crucial moment. But not letting go of guilt, shame, fear and blame about previous NOTwriting episodes will only use up your time and energy and stop you getting to the writing. I understand that some days this is easier than others. But even on the difficult days it doesn't stop this being true: you cannot change the past. Nobody can change what they did or did not write yesterday. Forward! (This might be a good time to read Section 1, Goals.)

THE LONE SCHOLAR

If you ask me to imagine someone writing my mind produces an image of someone sitting alone at a desk, holding a pen or typing at a keyboard. I am not alone: do an image search for 'writing' if you want to see how ingrained the idea of a lone scholar is in our culture. Even if you ask me to imagine *myself* writing, I will picture the back of my own head bent over a notebook or laptop silently committing words in an even flow. Even though I *know* that this is only a small part of my writing experience. Even though this is the part of writing that is the part I am least good at! Even though I know that this is not how the creative part of writing happens for me, it is where my head goes every time. I never picture me in a video call with my co-author at her standing desk in another country waving my hands in animated explanation of my ideas. I don't remember the times we have stood in seminar rooms, rearranging data or drawing on whiteboards together. I never see myself walking around my village puzzling through a paragraph in my head. I never think about all the hours I've spent co-writing in bright rooms or video meetings with colleagues. My head doesn't go to the seminars where I've explained my ideas to myself as I address the room. I don't see all the heated discussions in canteens, offices and corridors where I have made manifest the most elegant ideas in the moment of debate. Even though these are my real experiences of productive writing. Even though my experiences are about talk and movement and sharing with others and doing almost anything but physically writing, I only see the writing down part of writing. And I only see myself. When the most cursory glance at my outputs will vouch for this almost never being the case. Even when my co-authors aren't physically (or digitally) present I am writing to them and with them. Even when I am typing something alone in my study I am writing in a chain of drafts that have come from, will go to or be shared with others in a generative, iterative chain of writing and feedback cycles. Writing is a conversation and academic writing is by definition a community-oriented business. We need to question the idea of the lone scholar, because it can be as debilitating as it is misleading (see almost anything in this section).

DOING IT ALL YOURSELF

Inextricably linked to the notion of the lone scholar (maybe because of it) is the idea that we need to write our books and chapters and papers by ourselves. Some of the people I spoke to in this study were stuck because they were intent on doing it all themselves. From framing the problem to collecting, transcribing and analysing the data to writing up the references, we secretly feel that allowing others to help us is somehow cheating. Again the socialisation process around UK doctoral theses sets us up for the expectation that we should operate on our own and complete every stage of the research and writing by ourselves. This can make for a very long and lonely road. Almost everyone I spoke to found writing with others faster and less difficult and/or less soul destroying. Many people actually used the act of passing drafts or sections to others as either a way of setting meaningful deadlines or as a way of getting unstuck. Even those successful writers who had horror stories to tell about writing with others still preferred teams and/or found them a faster way to travel. See Section 2, Get a co-author.

WRITING IS BOTH A PUBLIC AND PRIVATE PROCESS

I've suggested that when we think of academic writing we think about somebody sat at their desk, typing. I think we have the wider world of writing to blame for this image of the lone writer, struggling away on a single piece of prose day in and day out. Academia is perhaps unique in the extent to which writing is a shared process. Very few fiction authors or poets collaborate, for example. In fact we know that the majority of academics write with others, and my research suggests that many have multiple things in progress at any given time. This made me wonder about whether it is the private or the public parts of our writing processes that contribute to the ways in which we get stuck. I know that the perfectionists (discussed in Perfectionism in this section) strive to retain the private part of their process where they have complete control and autonomy as long as they can. Their (not)writing processes are inherently designed to keep others out. The early discussion cycles of writing teams, on the other hand, seem to have the opposite effect of obliterating the private writing stage from the start of their writing process altogether. One interviewee I spoke with handwrote all her notes in a book while she was reading, not venturing on to a typed page until she had her first sentences of argument formed. The shift from handwriting to typing signified a shift from work that was for her eyes only to work that was ready to be shared within her writing partnerships. I have a sense that the faster we move from our private writing processes to our public ones, the faster, more creatively and more robustly our writing travels (see Section 2, Talk about writing).

CELEBRATION

I have been lucky. In my early years of writing I was surrounded by people who taught me to celebrate writing success. The first time I got a paper accepted for a 3* journal, my head of department whipped the letter out of my hand (yes, you used to get a letter in the post!), made a whooping noise and did a little dance in the corridor outside my office, waving it over his head and drawing others out of their offices to congratulate me. His warm and genuine reaction to my success has never left me. I try to pass the whooping down to others in my circle. Anyone in my circle who has confessed via email to having articles accepted in cool places will testify to receiving an emailed 'WooooooooooooHooooooooooooooooo' in return. This an is electronic notification of the wee dance I am doing for you. It is so easy not to celebrate. To concentrate on the other things that have not yet been submitted, finished, started. But you need to pause and notice your success. As well as offering my best whooping (a pale shadow of the original but meant nonetheless with genuine feeling), I also send my peers and students permission to feel smug. For a week. They mostly look at me as if I am mad, but you need to learn to enjoy that feeling and to stretch it out and revel in it.

I remember being invited down to the foyer of a very fancy business school where I worked, to celebrate the results of the national Research Assessment Exercise[5] in the 1990s where the school had done exceptionally well, securing a large amount of research funding and a great deal of national and inter-national prestige. The staff were raising their glasses to the Dean, who had written our submission, toasting his skill and application. As he raised his glass in return to thank them, the radiant smile slipped away from his face and he said, 'Oh no [or words to that effect], I will have to resign quick in case we don't do well next time and my epitaph is "The Dean who lost the 5*[6] rating"'. He never even made it to the bottom of his first celebratory glass before moving on to worry about the next submission (which was five years away), the next challenge. Even being declared the best school in the country wasn't enough to make him enjoy his celebration.

I know a department where they keep a bottle of champagne in the common room fridge. Whenever a member of staff gets an article in a swanky journal there is a knocking on doors, a rounding up of peers and the bottle is opened and shared to fête the author of the moment. I love that they are poised to celebrate. I love that the champagne is paid for by the department. I love that their expectation is that their staff will get in the best journals and at any moment they will need to band together and help them celebrate. We need to do more of this. Not to put pressure on people to achieve spots in high-ranking journals, nor to privilege some kinds of writing over others, but to remind us all to pause. To take it in, to enjoy writing success. Otherwise, we will all just rush on to the next starting line and begin the next race without accepting and enjoying the benefits of our labours (see Section 1, Rewards).

COMPETITION

It only makes sense to compete with others and view their success as detrimental to our own if academic success is limited. There may only be one academic promotion to be had in your department each year and if someone gets that it might mean that you can't. But there are a LOT of different ways to have a successful academic career and, really, if we are honest, academic success is open to us all. It is not scarce, so we don't need to fight over it.

If you get rejected from a specific journal it is not a good feeling. We have all been there. Without exception, my data show. Everyone gets rejections. I know journal editors with pretty fancy track records who have been rejected from their own journals. Gotta love double-blind reviewing! But there are endless chances to try again. To write it better and resubmit, or write something different and try again. The person in the office next door getting published in that same journal does not decrease your chances of getting in now, or in the future. In fact, if you can ask their advice and guidance on your manuscript it may even increase your chances of getting accepted next time.

And words. They are not scarce. In fact, it is my experience that words beget more words. The more you write, the more you will write more. After a while, what 'more' means will expand and, if you keep practising writing more, soon you will be able to write MORE. So when you sit down to write, try to focus not on the worries about what others are doing, or how much you need this article done so that you can let the writing happen. Elizabeth Gilbert famously promised her writing that she would never force it to make a living for her (2016, p. 140). As academics we would do well to protect our writing in a similar way and see whether we can get back to our sense of what is important and our need to say something about that, and set it free from the pressure of having to earn us promotions.

Focus away from the competition and focus instead on the words. Focus on the point that you are trying to make. The thing that you are keen to communicate. Focus on the words. And when someone else achieves a great thing, even if it is the very thing you want so badly for yourself, take a moment to enjoy their success and let them know you are impressed. Because there is plenty of success for us all. And the competition is making us all miserable. (See Section 2, Join a writing group.)

A WEE NOTE FOR ALL THOSE LOVELY PEOPLE STRUGGLING WITH THEIR DOCTORAL THESIS

My grandma got quite worried about me when my PhD funding ran out and I went to work as a research assistant to fund myself through the end game of my thesis. She couldn't understand how my time was up but I had not 'finished' my degree. When I eventually did get it complete, I sent it to the best proofreader in the business: my mum. It was just over 500 pages and I parcelled it up in the lid of a box of copier paper (which is one ream deep). My mum took it out to show my grandma. Instantly, Grandma understood what was going on. 'She was writing a book all this time. Why did nobody just say that?', and the mystery of not being 'finished' was solved for her. I am telling you this not because I want you to frighten old ladies with your theses, but because we mythologise the thesis. Every thesis. But especially our own. And that is probably one of the most dangerous things we can do if we want to get the damn thing finished. Try to remember: it's just a book.

Your PhD thesis is not your life work. I know that you want it to be perfect. I know it is difficult to give up on that idea. But you need to understand that:

1. it won't be perfect; and
2. that doesn't matter.

You will grow past it and write better things and learn that it was just an entry ticket to this crazy game we call academia. It will be huge. On the bookshelf. In your life for quite a few years. But it is just a book. It will have spelling errors. It will have at least half a chapter you should have left out and at least one underpinning premise that looks pretty optimistic with hindsight. A year after you graduate you will secretly hope that nobody ever reads it. I am telling you this not to devalue the thing. Or the journey. Or to downplay your struggle. I am hoping that if you catch a glimpse of it as 'just a book' then you can let go of all the jeopardy and hype and perfectionism and just write it. Also: there are some nice things in Section 6 on new ways to think about doctoral writing that you might like.

LAST WORD

Although the ideas in this section can help shift your *thinking* about being stuck, you will find that it always links back to parts of Sections 1 and 2, which are all the things that you could *do* to stop being stuck. This is because, even though the thinking is really helpful in changing our understanding – and as academics we can be naturally drawn to think (and think, and think, and think, and think, and sorry, what were we talking about?) – the key to getting unstuck lies in the doing. Writing is mainly doing, after all. So, although for many people the business of getting unstuck might begin by thinking differently, ultimately they will have to start doing things differently. That's why all the roads in this book lead back to Sections 1 and 2. Some folks will find their remedies there right away, others will need to deal with new thinking as well as new doing, but nobody can get unstuck without the doing.

Start Now:

Make an action plan of things to try
Make a list of folk who might help
Get curious about whether any of your writing beliefs are getting in your way

NOTES

1. See Glossary entry on Typos.
2. See Glossary entry on Research Excellence Framework.
3. See Glossary entry on Thesis.
4. See Glossary entry on Science and Engineering Research Council.
5. Before we had the Research Excellence Framework (see Glossary) we had the Research Assessment Exercise. Same nonsense, different name.
6. In those early days, the ranking went up to 5 and then 5* – this rank was very, very rare indeed.

4.   Improving your writing

This isn't really a book about how to write well. It is about how to get writing, write more and write more often. To paraphrase Ralph Keyes (2003), the hard part of that isn't getting your commas in the right place but getting your head there. But since you asked so nicely, here is my best advice about how to write better. First of all, if you are currently notwriting or NOTwriting, then I beseech you not to try to write better. Please. Just skip over this section and come back another day once you have got yourself unstuck. Worries about how good our writing is are really big for lots of us and, although perfectionism might seem cute when you are rehearsing your piano scales, it is not helpful for your writing. AT ALL. Have a look at Section 3, perfectionism instead. Go on. Off you go.

If, however, you are stuck with the 'how' of writing, or have copious drafts you are not sure how to move forward, then read on. This section is a brief overview of some ways that you can improve your academic writing. I didn't intend to write a section on improving your writing in this book, partly because striving to write in a particular way, or at a certain level, is a big part of being stuck for some people. People like me, who lean toward perfectionism, for example. However, when I was interviewing people who were endeavouring to do their academic writing in their second (L2), or even third (L3) languages, I found that not understanding 'how' to write academic English was part of their experience of being stuck. So this section is for all those lovely L2 and L3 folks, and the wonderful academics whose first academic reading and writing experiences are not in the same academic traditions as me, and anyone else who needs the rules made explicit so that they can take the crazy norms of academic writing into their own writing. (See Sword, 2017, ch. 6 for some great data from L2 scholars talking about writing in English.)

There are really only three ways to get better at writing. You are not going to like them, I am warning you now. OK, you might like the first one, which fits nicely into the 'virtuous avoidance' category for many academics:

1.   Reading.
2.   Writing.
3.   Feedback on your writing.

READING

Academic writing is a funny old thing. It is full of rules and conventions that we need to learn if our writing is to be accepted but, for the vast majority of us, nobody tells us what those rules are. It can feel a bit like a game of 'pin the tail on the donkey' for the uninitiated. There are a few epic supervisors out there with the time, energy and skills to give you a crash course in 'not like that, like this', but those are pretty rare. This is a really frustrating situation. People comment that your writing isn't in an appropriate style, or isn't academic in nature, or that your language is too informal, or that you need to develop a more scholarly voice, but they don't tell you (a) what exactly is wrong with what you have written or (b) how to fix it. I know this is maddening, but the truth is that it is not that those academics *won't* tell you, it is usually that they *can't* tell you. Because most of us learned what we know about academic writing by reading. In fact, if you grew up in the UK and are my age, you have never even formally learned to write English at all. Unless you studied a more structured language than English at school, you might not even know what the tenses and cases are called, although you use them with dexterity and can 'hear' when they are wrong. Whilst we may be able to say when someone else's writing is incorrect or inappropriate in a specific context, we can't say why or what it is that they need to do to fix it, despite being able to tell them with certainty what they should have written! So, don't be too hard on your writing mentors. They are not being secretive or difficult, they sometimes genuinely don't know how to tell you where exactly you are going wrong. They, like you, were never taught how to write in academese. They learned by reading.

The good news is that if we learned by reading, then so can you! Here are some adventures in academic reading that might help speed up the development of your academic writing. Reading can help your writing in two main ways: reading for content and reading for structure.

Reading for Content

First of all, read as much good work in your field as you can. Yes, I know this will take ages. It is an adventure, not a day trip. But it will always stand you in good stead. If there is a journal that you would love to be in, read loads of back issues. Every journal is an ongoing debate between hundreds of scholars, drawn out and interwoven over time. If you read work in the journals you aspire to you will start to register the nuances in the 'voice' used by the authors. Any parent whose children pronounce common words in their own language in ways used by people from a part of the world they have never been to, courtesy of Disney or YouTube, can testify to the power of your brain to absorb, assimilate and mimic different language styles. Keep reading. You don't need to do this all at once. Just keep it going. Paper by paper you will retrain your brain and your 'ear' for their preferred language and your writing will change.

Reading for Structure

Next, start reading for structure instead of content. This process is about trying to make the mechanics of someone else's writing explicit. Take a couple of papers that you really admire and look closely at the structure. How exactly are the arguments structured? How is evidence built up to make a point? Not just the explicit structure, denoted by headings and the ordering of sections, but the implicit structure. Every paragraph should make a single point. What is the point of every paragraph? How do these build into an argument? What understanding does the author convey of critique? Is it treated as a negative view of a phenomenon, or is there a balanced portrayal of strengths and weaknesses? Is it de rigueur to accept well-known theories at face value, or do they hold even the most widely accepted concepts up to the light and inspect their assumptions and discuss their limitations? If you start from the view that each word, sentence and paragraph has been crafted and positioned with great care, you can ask yourself: why? What exactly are the authors trying to do by choosing that expression or ordering the statements like this? Ask all of the questions! Focus on the how. Work out the 'writing conventions' of effective authors or the 'house style' of a specific journal from first principles. Then steal them!

You can also look at the referencing micro politics. Do the references always pay homage to the classics, or do they favour the cutting edge? Or maybe a balance of the two? Is their convention to cite only works in the immediate field, or do authors tend to cite widely, drawing in materials from across the disciplines? Does your favourite journal love loads of references to other works in their favourite journal? Journals love to self-cite even more than the most blowhard academic you know. Officially, it locates your paper within the ongoing debate they are fostering and demonstrates the relevance of your piece to their journal. Of course, it also impacts their impact factor, so make your own mind up about the purpose of such practices. Even if you think it is the latter, it probably helps if you comply with this aspect of house style, just as you would rigorously replicate their referencing conventions.

If you can make all these different clues to writing norms explicit for yourself by dissecting a couple of papers you'd love to have written, you can start adopting them in your own writing. Maybe not as you write your first draft, but you can certainly consciously introduce them as you edit. See Section 3, Writing is a single skill – which is of course a mad idea.

For an additional adventure: read the classics. Never cite something you haven't read. Even if it was written by people who are long dead. Even if everyone cites it. Even if you know what it says because you have read loads of other folks' opinions on it. If it is fundamental to what you are arguing, find it and read it for yourself. You would be amazed how often I have found really famous opinions to be slightly different than their widely accepted meanings.

A side note on the cleverness and complexity of some academic writing as showing off and keeping people out: if you have to read something 17 times whilst you press on your temples to understand something in your own discipline it is my view (and probably a controversial view) that it is not well written. If it is in another discipline, well, it is perhaps to be excused, but if it is in your own field then I suspect that this is writing that is about communicating how clever and sophisticated the authors are rather than explaining a new idea to as many folk as possible. Please don't be impressed by this. Please don't try to write like that. Please don't aspire to write only for the few. This is writing borne of insecurity and exclusivity. It is the kind of crazy game playing that might help us individually feel clever but collectively stops us walking forward together or at pace.

P.S. Reading about Writing

One of the things that has really helped me over the years is to realise that writing is writing is writing. It doesn't really matter if you are writing a doctoral thesis or a science fiction novel, the writing is a relatively similar process. This has two effects. The first is that we re-understand that writing is a creative process (see Section 1, Creativity). The second is that it opens up a whole new world of advice and support. One of my favourites is reading books about writing written by writers from other writing worlds. There are some fiction writers that have written magnificent accounts of their writing processes which I find both helpful and inspiring. My current favourite is Elizabeth Gilbert's *Big Magic*, but there is a list of other classics in Section 6. If you had offered me one of these (and people tried) the first time I was stuck, I would have rolled my eyes. I saw academic writing as entirely different from, for example, fiction. I thought that these writers had nothing to teach me. Looking back, I can see what that says about how little I knew of my craft, and how badly I needed academic writing to somehow be different from fiction. I really thought that writing a PhD thesis was a solely and uniquely intellectual endeavour and not a personal journey. I was dead wrong. Could not have been wronger. Try one. What's the worst that could happen?

The good news about all this reading is that it can be a good way to get unstuck. However, if you suspect yourself of setting up some gargantuan reading lists as a way of putting off the evil day when you will actually have to write, then you might be straying into sharpening pencils or even virtuous avoidance territory (see Section 1, Sharpening pencils).

WRITING

Yeah. Sorry about that. One of the most powerful ways of getting better at writing is to write more. You sure as hell won't get better by staring at blank pieces of paper, that I can guarantee (trust me, I have lost whole weeks of my life to this particular strategy). You might get better at the staring, but that is another story for another section. But if you can write something, anything, then two brand new opportunities arise: firstly, you can get practice in the thing you are trying to do better; and secondly, you can improve it.

Drafts

The first version you write of anything will be somewhere on the scale between rubbish and seriously mediocre. This is true for everyone. Don't mistake the first version of the thing that your co-author sends you for their first draft. Most of us never show anyone our first drafts. I only know this because of all the one-to-one work I have done over the years with people who are stuck with their writing. In order to help them I need to see the actual state of the thing they are writing. It typically takes me a couple of weeks to wrestle it off them so that we can begin. Those first weeks are spent talking about writing in general and how difficult I have found things in the past in order to build up enough trust to allow me into their actual writing process and show me the extent of the stuck (both in their writing and in themselves). So, I have seen more true first drafts than most, as many of us have only ever seen our own. But the first drafts are not rubbish because those folks are stuck or because they are notwriting, or indeed because they are poor writers. The first drafts are rubbish because they are FIRST DRAFTS. Nothing you see in print rattled off someone's keyboard looking like that. Nothing! Those articles have been through several rounds of internal review by each author privately (for me, this is typically two or three drafts but it can be up to six, depending on how tricky I find setting out my argument to be), and another couple of shared drafts by any or all of the writing team. They have probably been offered to colleagues to read and comment on before they even got submitted to a journal. Then they have been read and commented on by the journal editor and up to four reviewers, probably at least twice in the best journals. Many articles are not published in the first journal they were sent to, so you can multiply that whole thing by two or three more sets of comments and a whole lot more drafts. Even once they have been accepted, a copyeditor will check your grammar and references are strictly correct before it goes to a proof, which you can all check for final adjustments. So stop comparing your first draft to things published in top journals.

The opposite is also true, of course: don't kid yourself that because you have written out all the points you want to make that your first draft is in any way a 'finished' piece.

In order to conceptualise the drafting process and take account of it in their planning of writing, some people like to undertake drafts with different purposes (Brabazon, 2010). So, for example, one draft's purpose might be to check if every paragraph makes a single point. Another might be to flesh out all the references that you have spattered liberally through your text and put more in (or in my case, have a co-author take more out). If you have a brilliant mind but not a brilliant written style, one draft might be assigned to a co-author who could go through your draft and improve the flow or syntax. If you don't have co-authors or supervisors who you can ask to do this sort of thing, there is always the possibility of asking for professional support to address a specific weakness in your writing (see Section 3, Doing it all yourself, and Section 6).

Synthesis and Critique

Two of the hallmarks of academic writing are synthesis and critique. What I have noticed over the years is that lots of writers don't have a clear idea of what synthesis and critique actually *are*, and a whole lot more don't know *how* to achieve them in their own writing. Comments like 'lacks synthesis' and 'needs more critique' are almost ubiquitous in every kind of writing feedback from supervisor comments to reviews from swanky journals. These techniques are pretty much always missing from early drafts because they are not how we write naturally. I would recommend always checking your work for synthesis and critique but I would equally advise not trying to start with these but instead let them evolve (or deliberately evolve them!) through drafts.

Synthesis
If you ask me to tell you about my research, I will naturally launch into a story. The story will probably be from a single point of view (mine) and it will be almost entirely descriptive. Academic writing works the same way. If I am writing a literature review I will read every paper, one at a time, and then make notes on that paper. Once I am done I will read another and another (and if you are me, anotherandanotherandanotherandanotherandanother … see how to diagnose virtuous avoidance in Section 1, Sharpening pencils!), filling up my notebook with scribbled notes. When I eventually sit down to write a first draft

of that literature review, I will write about each of the papers in turn. Here is a fictional example using made-up references:

> Wang (1962) argues that cats are almost certainly orange.
> Johansson (1982) undertook a large-scale study which shows that cats are black, white or black and white and mostly asleep.
> Musa's (1974) earliest work demonstrates that cats are grey and temperamental.

The first draft of my review might look like this:

> Wang (1962) argues that cats are almost certainly orange. Musa's (1974) earliest work demonstrates that cats are grey and temperamental. Johansson (1982) undertook a large-scale study which shows that cats are black, white or black and white and mostly asleep.

This is what I like to call the 'he said, she said' draft. I have grouped all the writing on cats together. Here I have used the study dates as an organising factor. The voice here is the reported voice of the original authors.

The sixth draft of my review, in which I have deliberately introduced synthesis, might look like this:

> Various commentators have found cats to be orange (Wang, 1962), grey (Musa, 1974), black, white or black and white (Johansson, 1982). Whilst some studies reported that they were temperamental (Musa, 1974), others commented on how much they slept (Johansson, 1982).

Here it is the argument that is driving the order of the citations and the voice is not the reported voice of others, but mine. We have introduced the voice of the writer writing *this* piece.

If you'd like to see the difference that synthesis makes, compare Section 6 (which is in the style of an annotated bibliography) with a literature review from a published paper.[1] Neither style is 'better' than the other, it's just that they are doing very different jobs.

Critique

In everyday speech, the term 'critical' has come to mean something negative. In academic terms, though, it means something broader. To critique something is to point out its weaknesses, but also its strengths and its underlying assumptions. I sometimes think we restrict ourselves to considering weaknesses because they are by far the easiest to find! Good critique is balanced. Great critique can also reveal and even challenge the norms of the research traditions which produced the work.

Sometimes, the reluctance to critique comes from a good old-fashioned lack of confidence. It is hard to critique the work of others if you don't feel your own legitimacy as an academic writer (aka your head is full of 'who the hell do you think you are to judge X?'). I also want to acknowledge that critique is difficult for scholars who have learned their writing skills in cultures where the critique of specific groups of others (such as published scholars or elders) or disagreeing publicly is not encouraged. These deep-seated norms are hard to get past. It takes commitment and practice but can feel deeply uncomfortable and even dangerous for some. Sometimes the idea of examining the positives, negatives and assumptions of others' work is more approachable than thinking of critique as being negative, and has unlocked the habit of critique for some scholars I have worked with.

The seventh draft of my review, then, might pick up on some weaknesses of the body of work:

> Early scholars in the field studied a limited range of attributes and were predominantly limited to cat colour (Wang, 1962; Musa, 1974, Johannson, 1982).

It could mention some strengths:

> Over time, studies included a wider range of factors and larger sample sizes, leading to a more complex and comprehensive picture of the cat (Wang, 1962; Musa, 1974, Johannson, 1982).

And it could even consider some of the underpinning assumptions of the field:

> Although the early emphasis on cat colour has become balanced in modern work with consideration of a range of behavioural factors, it is still clear to see that the field is constrained by its reliance on structured observational methods which lend themselves to the reporting of physical and behavioural characteristics.

Doing synthesis before critique helps you to stand back and look at the way an argument or line of research in a field has been developed rather than focusing on what is wrong with specific papers. The reason we love these techniques so much is that they 'add value' to the field. Anyone could read the same stack of papers and report or describe what is in them, but without synthesis and critique, they just turn into a stack of sentences. This saves the reader the time needed to read the whole paper, but adds very little of the reviewer. Synthesis adds organising and sensemaking skills. Critique adds the opinion of the reviewer. The reviewer's voice is often (but not always) signalled by the lack of references, especially if the critique follows a synthesis, as it does in my draft 7 above. Now the stack of sentences has formed into an argument. To find your academic 'voice' you need to practise adding synthesis and critique and stepping into your own story of what is happening in your field.

This isn't easy but it is also not magical or mysterious: it is just a matter of practice. Try taking a paper you love and three colours of highlighter pen and mark up a couple of pages. Highlight all the description in one colour, the synthesis in a second and use the third for critique. A good paper will have all three. Probably in descending order of magnitude. Or maybe with more description in some sections and more critique in others. You will soon find that synthesis can be an implicit critique and that these can work together in some interesting ways (but that is another story for another day!). Look and see how the writers you admire use these three techniques to build argument and structure their work. Now, take the last draft of your own work and mark it up in the same way (or ask a writing buddy to do it). Lacks synthesis? Needs more critique? You know what to do!

P.S. Please read more than three sources!

P.P.S. Please, please don't read as many as me!

FEEDBACK

In the space of my 30 year academic career I have gone from a perfectionist doctoral student with my arm round my jotter to a feedback junkie. Sure, you can improve your writing without feedback from other people but it is definitely slower. It is also much, MUCH easier to have colleagues embody a load of slightly different perspectives than it is to get there yourself.

Building on the points in the last section, I also know people who make a very high-level draft (a PowerPoint draft, if you like) of their paper to make sure that the main points are there in the right order. I rarely submit a piece of work that has not been read by colleagues and also presented at an academic conference. If the timing is wrong for a conference, I have been known to wrangle a departmental seminar, either in my own university or in one I am visiting for some other reason, just to try out my ideas. Some people conceptualise their first drafts as tickets to feedback. Once you have something, you can share it. Once you share it, you can get ideas about how successful it is as a piece of communication and improve it.

The truth is that receiving feedback and dealing with it is an integral part of academic life. Virtually nothing is published without having been changed in response to feedback. If you want to be published you will need to learn the art of responding to feedback. So, seek out feedback and get used to dealing with it.

One of my most influential writing mentors told me that when you get a stinking review you are allowed 24 hours of outrage (HOW could they say THAT. They CLEARLY haven't even read it properly ...), followed by a week of sulking (nobody understands what I am saying, I will never be able to do this, it is so hard to get qualitative/cross-disciplinary/educational [delete as applicable] stuff published …) and then after that you have to take a deep breath and look in the reviews for the things you can improve and the perspectives you hadn't considered and rewrite.

One strategy for taking the emotional sting out of the feedback process and unlocking the 'how' of academic writing (and to be gifted the eye of the reviewer) is to get involved in reviewing yourself. By that I do not mean 'unleash a tirade of negativity on yourself about the difference between the thing you have produced on paper and the shiny thing in your mind's eye'. I mean 'volunteer to be a reviewer for a conference or a journal'. Lots of communities welcome help with this. If you have never done it before, ask someone else to do it with you the first time or just to check your draft. Ask the conference organiser for feedback on your feedback. Ask the journal editor for a review of your review. Read lots of academic book reviews if these are published in your discipline's academic journals. There are even some great papers on how to review for journals and how to respond to reviewers (see Section 6).

Rejection from journals is the cruellest and most soul-destroying form of feedback. But the best journals have a rejection rate well in excess of 90% across the disciplines, so if you submit things to journals you will get rejected. It happens to everyone. Everyone. The more prolific and successful a writer you are, the MORE rejections you will get, not less. Give it a week, and then try to see it as feedback. If no feedback is offered, ask for some. Let it fuel your improvement, not stop you in your tracks.

LAST WORD

Writing is something we can all learn and something we can all improve. Don't fall for the idea that writing well is a mysterious talent that someone is born with (or not born with). Read more, write more and get (and implement!) as much feedback on your writing as you can and your writing will improve, I promise. Maybe not as quickly as you'd like, but definitely in the general direction of 'better'.

NOTE

1. See an open-access version of a paper (McDonald, 2005) which is more or less just a literature review that I wrote many years ago; read from page 9: Seonaidh McDonald, Studying actions in context, https://rgu-repository .worktribe.com/OutputFile/294295.

5. Institutional problems (and what you might do about them)

Every department, at any given time, will have a few folk who are stuck with their writing. If, however, a whole department is notwriting or if their combined outputs are dwindling in scope, number, impact or quality, then it might be time to look carefully at the institutional infrastructure and/or culture to see if some of the stuck has a common denominator.

If you are reading this book because you are trying to get a group of folks unstuck then there is some advice here to help you do that. If, however, you are trying to get unstuck and you might see the face of your institution or department in the mirrors I am holding up here, there may be little you can personally do to shift some of these issues. If unhelpful cultural norms are mosquitoes in your day: find the others. Make your corner of the world as kind and bright as you can. If it is becoming unbearable: do those things, but also keep yourself safe. Either way: don't get disheartened and do try to write yourself up or out of your current situation.

SCARCITY

We operate from a scarcity mindset. Now, there is plenty of genuine scarcity in the higher education context these days. Changes to the funding model over the last two decades have reduced the amount of funding at the same time when changes in access to higher education mean a larger number of students to teach. Government funding can definitely be said to be more scarce for this generation of UK academics than it was for the last, for example, and I know this is true for many countries. The lowest staff–student ratios which used to be wielded as a badge of honour by the best institutions are now so high as to no longer be published. Academic time is also finite and this commodity is often vehemently wrangled over at an individual, departmental and university level. There are a finite number of students (who either pay fees or bring government funding, depending on where you live) for the universities to fight over. A course offer from one institution accepted by a specific student means they will not attend the other institutions for which they hold offers. So, whilst students are many, competition is still necessary because they represent money and money is scarce.

Somehow, though, we have allowed the idea of scarcity to permeate every fibre of our culture until we, as institutions, as individuals, operate as if all of our resources were scarce. Of course we need funding, students, a specific classroom at 10am on a Tuesday morning, a particular post, seats on a specific committee, pages in a specific journal (real quick) before the hammer falls on the next career-defining deadline, all of which we might realistically compete over. But we have forgotten the resources that we have that are not scarce. That are, in fact, the opposite of scarce.

Ideas are not scarce. Ask any academic who perceives themselves as struggling with their writing and I will guarantee that their problem is not that they don't have enough ideas for things to write about. In fact, their problem is more likely to be too may ideas to choose from, too many ideas to do justice to in one lifetime of academic writing. If you are short of ideas, please just stop the first academic you see and ask for some of their spare ones and you will shortly have a lovely long list of things you might pursue.

Words are not scarce. They are an endless, reusable resource. Once they get going, they can be self-perpetuating like one of those kinetic structures that twirls for days after a puff of wind.

Curiosity is not scarce. The human brain is a meaning-seeking, pattern-divining muscle that is capable of questioning and opening to more questioning, on and on through glittering new perspectives, frames and reframes. Who, where, what, when, why and how in infinite permutations.

Kindness, respect, care, love, trust, joy. Not scarce. We make these by making them. We multiply them by sharing them. We can make as much of them as we want. Which raises some very interesting questions indeed about the cultures in some departments.

I don't know about you, but I did not join academia to get on a particular committee or to teach in a particular classroom. I'm here for the ideas. For the sharing and growing and understanding of ideas. I didn't bargain on kindness or joy, but it has made all the rest quite splendid.

If your department is at loggerheads it is because there is deep-seated competition fuelled by an idea of scarcity which is making everyone feel insecure. The role of good academic leaders is to hold space for their people so that they can have the freedom and confidence to do the things they were hired to do: great teaching and research. Not pit them against each other by promoting a scarcity culture to see whether the resulting fights to the death will catapult the group into new levels of achievement. I guess it might in the short term, but only if you are happy with the idea that your staff are disposable, because by next year you are going to need a whole other set of loggerheads to be at. Exhausting, pointless and unsustainable, even if you can convince yourself that it is ethical.

Can we stop with the scarcity thing now, please? I know that the lack of money is hard. Let the accountants deal with the money. Let's try to collectively remember why we are here (to push back the boundaries of knowledge; to inspire a generation). Our scarcity fetish and the competition it inspires drives us into league tables, h-indexes, cliques, back biting, imaginary hierarchies and a whole load of completely unnecessary unhappiness. We can subvert all these drives to competition by simply resisting the notion of scarcity and acting accordingly (see Section 2, Join a writing group).

OPEN-PLAN OFFICES

OK, people. Listen up. Academic writing does not happen in open-plan offices. Quite apart from being inhumane and soul destroying, they are not places in which people who may already be struggling to write can achieve flow. They are sold to universities as being 'modern' and 'increasing communication', but the only thing they are is cheap: increased academics per square foot. Have a look at the research if you don't believe me (Brennan, Chugh & Kline, 2002; Danielsson & Bodin, 2008; Van Marrewijk & Van den Ende, 2018). All that will happen is that the academics will make use of the one freedom they have left, which is to work anywhere, and leave. Some of them will lurk in the library in its quiet hours, some will type on laptops in the university's eating places but many will simply go home. So much for the cross-fertilisation of ideas and open communication between peers. Of course, this has the added benefit of keeping the heating and lighting costs down because you can simply switch it off in the open-plan areas as nobody is using them. So if cheapness is your goal then go right ahead with your soft-coloured, slightly padded room dividers. If research of any kind is what you want to achieve, and scholarly writing in particular, you're going to need walls. If your institution has already downgraded its academics to tiny desks with tinier barriers between them, you need to tackle this urgently before writing can happen and before a research culture can grow. You need to provide spaces with PCs where people can write. The spaces should not be tiny, windowless cupboards. They should be beautiful, spacious, have the best views on campus and be bookable by the half day. If this is your department, you need to find somewhere you can write. Start by checking out your library.

PRESENTEEISM

Just about the same point in the history of academic buildings that some universities started to make everything open plan and all the academics wandered off somewhere else to write, some of them also dabbled in 'efficiency' measures in an effort to control their staff. As the idea of academic work changed from something a bit odd to something a bit more managerial, some departmental heads (the same ones who believed that open-plan offices would increase collaboration and create synergistic efficiencies) were dismayed by the emptiness of their shiny new floor layouts. They assumed that if academics were not sitting at their tiny workspaces then they were not 'working'. In fact, the tiny workspaces were not (never have and will not ever be) working. But anyway, having read their human resources handbooks they issued decrees that insisted that employees would work in the office five days each week and between the hours of 9am and 5pm. That way, they thought, everyone will be in at the same time, and all that superefficient collaboration will be bound to happen; before you know it we will have doubled our output in half the time. Some even asked people to sign out if they went off site or ask for permission to work at home. Loopholes duly closed. Except all that happened is that the academics felt a breach of trust and respect. They did not come in, but they started to not come in furtively. A culture of presenteeism was born. People left their screens on and their jackets on their chairs so it looked like they were somewhere in the building, but had just stepped away from their desk for a moment. When they came in for afternoon meetings they did not bring coats or bags so that nobody would realise that they had just arrived for the day and their colleagues couldn't tell if they were off home or just popping to the toilet. When these kinds of conditions are formed, less writing is done, not least because so much energy has to be put into the presenteeism. These deserts of quietly buzzing screens and artfully arranged desktops make the chances of collaboration zero. Coercing people to undertake creative processes within certain times and spaces is unrealistic. All it inspires them to do is return your lack of trust and respect in spades.

Presenteeism is a battle for control. Managerial attempts to control academic work are deeply hated because academics value freedom and autonomy. Many of them are here because they don't want to be told what to do. Many of them do their teaching and admin in daylight hours and then give up their evenings, weekends and holidays to do their research and writing. When management insists that they are in a specific place between 9am and 5pm they imply that only what is (a) done in that building and (b) done between those hours is 'work'. It is implied that 'if I can't see you, you are not working'. It suggests that measures are required to make people work more or work better. Exhausted folks, who are working as much as they possibly can already, tend to be insulted by the implication that they are not doing enough or not doing it properly. This can lead to a culture which totally undermines writing practices. There are some great texts on managing knowledge workers and clever people that can give good suggestions of a more promising approach (I like the idea of a strengths perspective as set out in the work of Don Clifton [see Rath, 2007] and Andy Woodfield [2021], but there are lots of interesting things you could read in this broad area). The main idea is to treat people as individuals with different perspectives, priorities, proclivities and geniuses, rather than to get them to comply with a single idea of being an academic, or do a single kind of academic work in a specific way.

If you have a culture of presenteeism then it could be that what you have is a relationship between academics and management that is characterised by a lack of trust. Trust building is hard because it is a process of getting closer to people who you start out perceiving as having either damaging or derogatory motivations towards you. The truth is that their view of you (and vice versa) is more likely to be very limited than necessarily negative. It is entirely possible that you (and/or they) are operating from stereotypes (academics are lazy; human resources people are divisive; theory is irrelevant in the real world; management only care about money. Shall I go on?) rather than any actual firsthand knowledge of *you* as a person. But get closer you must. Step forward into the paradox (enter sci-fi theme tune of your choice) that to build trust you must bring trust. Trust yourself, trust the process, trust that you must in fact be mistaken that she has absolutely no redeeming features and/or no ability to do any of the work that is necessary here. Trust, trust, trust. And begin. And if you want to stand on the sidelines insisting that *they* trust you and step forward first … I'm just going to leave that with you. Come back when you are ready to break the spiral. Because trust is always a spiral of reciprocity and the one you are standing in is either an upward spiral of trust or a downward spiral of doom. Your choice. Your move.

I know it's hard. Really hard.

I know they started it.

I know they are more senior/more responsible/more to blame/behaved more badly than you [delete as applicable] so they should be the ones to start the repair.

I know you are doing your best already and you are tired. I see you.

I know you tried this before and they spat it back in your face.

I know.

Still.

Your move.

RESTRICTING RESEARCH AREAS

For lots of people, it is really hard to write. To write at a high level is really very hard indeed. It means draft after draft, of the same piece, over and over. It means reading an indeterminate amount of stuff (which doesn't have the common courtesy to even stand still while you write about it, but instead keeps moving, dammit). Sometimes on your own with little or no feedback or encouragement. Unless you count your charming spouse asking whether it is finished yet every time you emerge bleary eyed from your study. This is always encouraging. Sometimes, for a big or difficult project, it means being locked in this process year after year. So, why do we do it? For some of my respondents it was the challenge. Like someone determined to run a marathon. Some people just show up wherever there are big, difficult things to be done for the sheer love of the big and difficult. 4* journals (see Research Excellence Framework [REF] in the Glossary) are like mountains for some folks; they must climb them simply because they are there. Other people are ambitious and want promotion, tenure, success. The top journals are a huge stamp of approval for your work and for many collecting those stamps is a tangible way to feel like they are moving onwards and upwards. Personally, I am a self-development junkie and have an insatiable need to be a little bit better and a little bit better. Some folks I spoke to are keen to join the debate. They are either driven to drive knowledge forward or to make their mark, have their say and leave a legacy. Immortality through citations. Lots of people want to solve problems: theoretical puzzles; practical issues; or mismatches between academy and practice. They are motivated by intellectual curiosity or the wish for change and improvement in anything from formulae to rulings of the United Nations. They are also striving for better, but the focus of their striving is external rather than internal. But do you know what no one mentioned, not one person, not a single soul? Departmental strategy. Nobody puts themselves through the rigours of writing (whether they love it or not) in order to deploy a deep-seated wish for their department to meet targets. So, when departments try to make the game about the department itself rather than about either the individual or the discipline, all the motivation to write falls away. When departments try to force people to research in specific areas it seems that people get sad or angry or leave. This can be a staged process which plays out over a period of time (angry, sad, leave; leave, sad, angry) or it can happen overnight. Newsflash: sad, angry and former members of your department are not doing their best writing for you. See also frightened or demeaned scholars who are beaten with their own lack of progress. Threat is probably the fastest way to drain every single sparkle out of the writing process for people and slow them right down or stop them forever. The only person writing hard in this situation is the person motivated by the determination to write their way out of your institution as quickly as possible.

Strategically developing your research as a community is a great idea. You can focus on developing areas over time through recruitment and internal funding, if you want a strategy of excellence in a specific (or as is becoming common, just any) area. In the short term, you need to focus on developing everyone from where they currently stand, both in terms of skill and subject matter. Even if it looks like a jumble sale encyclopaedia of arbitrary themes. Better (and faster) to help the people you have shine in their own idiosyncratic ways whilst you bring your plan to establish the Welsh Centre of Excellence in International Cat Trading to fruition, because it will give you a lovely research culture which will attract all the lovely cat-trading experts to you in due course. There is no turning on a dime or any other currency here. Make no mistake, a group of academics is harder to change course than a tanker where at least a third of the occupants are rowing in a random, and changing, but opposing direction at any given time. This is going to take some time. Settle down and bring cake for everyone.

RESTRICTING WRITING FORMATS

Academics predominantly write for other academics. Evans and Smith (2019), for example, asked nearly 600 academics across the globe and the disciplines about their writing and found that articles for journals and conference papers were their most common output types. This holds in studies of what formats are reported to be 'productive outputs' in an African context (Uwizeye et al., 2021), although textbooks come a close third, suggesting more value placed on writing for students by African scholars. One of the reviewers of this book noted that when I write about writing, I most often write about writing papers. Journal articles. And she is right. Because that is what I mostly write and because, in my discipline, that is what has become the most important kind of academic writing. Of course, I could add in a glib footnote that suggests that when I discuss papers, the same more or less applies to all kinds of academic output. Which it does, more or less. And it is also true that a great number of disciplines have become obsessed with the journal article, setting so many of us off on paper-writing paths, that if you are stuck with your writing, then statistically speaking you are most likely to be stuck with writing a paper. So, I could just point that out and hope that she doesn't mind my sleight of hand. But she points to a very interesting assumption that I have made which is that getting stuck doesn't vary across different kinds of output for any given academic. And although this mostly holds true in my experience, in that I have been stuck with theses and blogs and book chapters and journal articles and research notes and reviews and editorials[1] in much the same way, it is not true for this book. So I am left wondering whether each of us has a format that suits us best. Where we are less liable to be stuck. Is there something about the different length, density of references, voice or format of different kinds of text that means that some will come to us more naturally than others? I don't know. What I definitely know is that not all ideas or arguments lend themselves to the journal article. Our best writing is not always done when we are addressing the three other scholars in our field. The challenge of different approaches to explaining yourself to different audiences can be a creative and instructive one. Maybe as well as advocating changing projects when you are stuck, I should recommend changing your audience. If we all just write articles intended for each other, our disciplines will certainly lose their vitality as novel perspectives become harder and harder to see. If we insist that our team only writes articles we may at best be restricting their creativity and communication and at worst be accelerating them towards being stuck. If people are writing, then celebrate. There is a place for all the different kinds of output in every faculty. Ranking them will simply give you less to count, not more.

TOWARDS BEING UNSTUCK AS A DEPARTMENT

Changing a culture is a difficult and long-term challenge. That doesn't mean you can put it off, it means you need to start right away. If you look around at the institutional setting and see some of the barriers you will find ideas to overturn them.

If you are recruiting, look for people who have a track record of getting other folk writing, and not just a track record of their own splendid outputs.

If you have a training budget (I know, remember them?!), invest in an early-career researcher who hasn't quite got their first paper out of their doctoral thesis. Or a mid-career researcher who seems to lack confidence.

If you have a conference budget, pay for conferences for the less established scholars, so that they can make networks and bump into like-minded peers in the bar. You might unlock a lifetime partnership of successful writing. Just choose one person a year and see what happens.

If you have a sabbatical scheme, consider giving a sabbatical to someone who used to write lovely things but has been stuck for several years. Oddly, sabbaticals are often won on the merit of those with the highest outputs getting them first. Buck the trend. Take a chance on someone. It might not pay off, but then again, you might revitalise a career and find yourself a grateful and inspired partner in crime to help you tackle the change in research culture. Plus, a success story to convince the grownups that you are not in fact completely mad.

If you have open-plan offices, make some kind of bookable writing space. Make it as lovely as you can. Let folks book it in advance (not too far in advance) and have it to themselves for a half day.

If you have a staff room, let it be known that you will be in there at a specific time every week (I know of a department who did this every day!) to talk about what you are writing and how it is going, and invite anyone who is vaguely interested to come and do the same. Invest in a coffee machine. Bring cake!

Also, let people write where they want. If they produce well in a café or in the library or in their pyjamas at home, try to allow for that and be flexible because this varies so much from person to person.

If you have a spare administrator for even half a day per week, ask them to take on some research support tasks, like formatting references or proof-reading manuscripts. Or you could have them do some of the admin tasks for an individual who is struggling to find time to complete a time-sensitive, key output. Could he update their tutorial attendance logs from last week? Send out a reminder about a staff seminar? Upload some slides onto the electronic learning platform? Or turn that crumpled pile of receipts into an immaculate expenses claim form? What's on the 'to do' list that could be done by someone else? If you have any slack in the system at all, use it to remove some of the tiny, cumulative administrative tasks that surround your researchers on every side and buy them some time and headspace.

If you have some successful writers in your group, sit them down and ask them if there are ways they could help others who are stuck. Some people might want to give a workshop on responding to reviewers, or structuring a literature review. Others might feel they could mentor someone in their field. I've seen a really successful volunteer take a series of workshops (with homework!) which took a small group of inexperienced and/or stuck scholars from conference paper or thesis chapter to submitted journal article over the course of several weeks, step by step. Helping others isn't for everyone, and even if they are willing, it won't always work out, but at the very least you can ask people to talk to colleagues about what they are writing and how it is going, to foster a more open and engaged environment for writing. If you don't have successful writers in your midst, invite some to come and speak to individuals or groups to share their war stories and be generally inspiring!

If you have no budget but you do have some time and energy to address this (or can find someone who has) then try speaking to people individually and figure out with them what might help. Or gather a group of people together to co-write in a meeting room on a Wednesday afternoon every few weeks. Sit down and write with them. Order tea and coffee and bring gorgeous biscuits for the breaks. Whether you work with people one to one or in groups, it is important to be open about your own writing process and start conversations about writing to break the silence we have collectively built up around this stuff.

If you have none of the resources on this list then it might be time to ask for some.

If you have a workload model, include writing! It is time to stop treating academic writing as if it is a luxury item that people can do in their spare time and/or after all the other things have been done. Academic writing is work. If you want increased outputs, schedule them in! If you can timetable for people in ways that are sympathetic to blocking time for writing in a day or week or term or even a year, experiment with that for people who are keen to write but loaded up with other commitments.

Above all: be open, be patient, be trusting and don't to forget to celebrate their successes.

LAST WORD

Last word for folks trying to get a whole group of academic writers unstuck: there are some folks who have more barriers to writing than others. The parents, the carers, the folks supporting extended family, the neurodiverse, the physically disabled, the mentally ill, the folks from difficult situations and less privileged backgrounds and the folks with genders, orientations and ethnicities that they do not see equally represented (or openly represented) in the academy when they look around themselves for role models. It isn't as easy for everyone to be inspired to aspire to be a white, middle-class bloke. Some of these folks have more practical barriers than others. Some have more barriers of spirit or focus. If you want to support more writing then seek out all the possible barriers a person might have with empathy and care in your heart and see what you can do to lift them. Level the playing field where you can. Where you can't, judge their writing in the context of their true situation, not what you'd like or expect it to be.

Last word for individual academic writers: academics are a pretty mobile tribe and so moving institutions is often seen as the answer for any given individual faced with the situations described in this section. If you are looking for a new job and you want to see whether prospective departments will be genuinely good environments for your research and academic writing then you could:

- Look at the current staff: How long have they been there? Have they been promoted in their own institution? Are only certain kinds of folks promoted? Do only certain kinds of folks have research outputs? Do the management team have vibrant and current publication records? If you are in a locale with national research reviews, are all the people from the last review still around? Do staff hold research funding? What proportion of the staff have doctorates? Do they all supervise doctoral students? Are there any post-doctoral researchers employed on research projects?
- Look at the academic writing support: Do they have academic writing training for early-career folks? Is there a writing group? Is there a seminar series with internal and/or external speakers? Is there a sabbatical scheme? Is there a mentoring scheme?
- Look at the outputs: Are they widely spread out across the majority of colleagues, or all done by a handful of folks? Do they write with each other? Do they write with their doctoral students? Is there a wide range of differ-

ent kinds of research topics represented? Have they hosted an academic conference? Do they get research funding?

Many of these can be interpreted in more than one way, of course, but taken together they can paint a picture of the kind of setting it would make for your academic writing. Some departments have a whole host of positive research indicators from the lists above, but are really competitive and have a culture of in-fighting and overwork that might make many of us miserable, for example. High outputs don't guarantee lovely human beings any more than a lack of outputs necessarily means the environment is toxic. You are a researcher. So use your skills to get a feel for what is happening. Speak to folks who work there, doctoral students who study there and folks who used to work there, look on websites like Glassdoor[2] for red flags. Take absolutely everything with a pinch of salt and triangulate relentlessly. Use the bibliometric databases to check out who is writing what with whom and whether people only stay for one paper or write there for a decade. Every university has its own special brand of nonsense going on; none of them are perfect. But if you can find one whose nonsense doesn't make you sad or angry then you have set the stage for a more positive relationship with your academic writing.

NOTES

1.   I have only never been stuck with textbook or popular science book writing because I have never written a textbook or a popular science book!
2.   www.glassdoor.co.uk/index.htm.

6. Resources

BOOKS ABOUT ACADEMIC WRITING

There are lots of great texts about academic writing. This is not a comprehensive list (if you'd like one of those, Sword [2017] has an excellent one), but it is a list of the ones I like best, speak about with folks who are stuck and recommend to my students.

Jensen, J. (2020). *Write No Matter What: Advice for Academics.* University of Chicago Press.

This is a friendly, kind and helpful book. Jensen is an experienced, passionate and practical advocate for academic writing and for supporting both students and faculty with her insights, in real life as well as in this book. It is authentic and beautifully written and makes me feel as though I have sat down in her office and shared my worries over a cup of tea. She offers a great deal of sound advice. Her perspective is that academic writing is a craft and that we are all apprentices. I particularly like her use of the 'ventilation file' described in chapter 4 to overcome resistance (see Section 3, Resistance). She also outlines some pretty useful reverse-planning techniques to both work out how you actually spend your time and then plan how you will henceforth make use of the different kinds of time you have available. She uses these exercises to find writing time in the business-as-usual semester and to plan writing, rest and recuperation slots into non-teaching times and sabbaticals.

Sword, H. (2017). *Air & Light & Time & Space: How Successful Academics Write.* Harvard University Press.

This book is the outcome of an international, mixed-methods study of academic writing habits. It is a book about how academic writers actually write. It is based on 100 interviews with academics from a wide range of countries and disciplines and 1223 questionnaires which have been completed by Sword's workshop attendees. It represents the practices of folks at all levels of the academy and all stages of their careers. Sword has built a model on the basis of this broad and deep data set which uses a house metaphor and identifies four pillars of practice: behavioural habits; artisanal habits; social habits; and emotional habits (BASE). You can work out the shape of the foundation of your own house on her website.[1] The book offers two things in spades: a phenomenal amount of data on how people do their writing that showcases the wild variety of ways in which we write; and an encyclopaedic array of references to what must be lists of every book ever written on academic writing. Both the data and literature are organised around her BASE model, making this a useful source book for you if you are looking for lists of new habits to try or more books to read on academic writing.

Clark, T., Wright, M., & Ketchen, Jr., D. J. (Eds) (2016). *How to Get Published in the Best Management Journals*. Edward Elgar Publishing.

This book is full of extremely sage advice. It is a bit like eavesdropping at the bar of a management conference and hearing all the old hands telling each other their stories. You could spend a whole career in this discipline and never manage to sit down with so many stellar scholars and hear their best advice and insider accounts. Some of the advice about specific journals or subfields will be more useful to management scholars than to other folks, but some of the advice is more universal in nature. There is a really good section on navigating the review process (but see also chapter 7 by William Starbuck). I also really like Mike Wright's chapter 6 on sustaining an academic career.

Oshima, A., & Hogue, A. (2007). *Introduction to Academic Writing*. Pearson/Longman.

If you would like an old-school introduction to *exactly* how to write a paragraph or form a sentence, then this is the book for you. No question is left undiscussed and no detail is too small to be explained. It even has stuff to practise if homework is your thing. If you are undertaking the heroic task of writing this stuff in your second, third or fourth language (first of all: respect!), this book will decode all of the nonsense that is the madness of the English language. I'm not saying you'll suddenly like academic English, I'm definitely not saying it will make any sense, I'm just saying you'll know what it is and be able to replicate it!

Wolcott, H. F. (2008). *Writing Up Qualitative Research*. Sage.

Qualitative research brings its own joys and challenges and this is by far the best text I have ever read on how to write about it. It is a masterclass from a true master. There are still a lot of journals that offer direction on how to format and sequence research writing by assuming that the assumptions of quantitative research will be able to be applied to writing about all kinds of studies. These have got fewer over the course of my career, but it is still really lovely for me to read a whole book on academic writing where narrative data are considered 'normal' (pun intended). There is a really useful section that distinguishes between analysis and writing, which can be very blurred for qualitative researchers in a way that makes it really hard to see which part they are actually stuck with (Wolcott reflects on how seeming to be stuck in one can actually be a sign of being stuck with the other). He writes in the first person, making his accounts feel both personal and powerful and he advocates we do the same in our academic writing. There are also some reflective exercises at the end of each section, which make for good discussion and/or practice.

RESOURCES FOR FOLKS WITH EXTRA WRITING CHALLENGES

Wallbank, A. J. (2022). *Academic Writing and Dyslexia: A Visual Guide to Writing at University*. Taylor & Francis.

Online, you can also listen to Adrian Wallbank talk about inclusion and neurodiversity at UCL.[2] Both students and their supervisors will find a wealth of resources at PhDisabled.[3] Scholarstudio have curated a really useful range of resources.[4] The ADHD Collective has published a blog for students on essay writing.[5] They also run co-working sessions for ADHD folks (click on 'Services' to see these).

PAPERS ON THESIS WRITING

Kamler, B., & Thomson, P. (2008). The failure of dissertation advice books: Toward alternative pedagogies for doctoral writing. *Educational Researcher*, 37(8), 507–514.

I love this paper. If reading 'how to' books that specialise in two-dimensional, context-free recommendations (make a plan, stick to your plan …) makes you feel inadequate and cross at the same time, I think you will love it too. It is a genius explanation of why I have those reactions to one-size-fits-all advice for doctoral researchers (any researchers!). You will also find signposts to a wider debate on doctoral writing and some recommendations for where to find more holistic, nuanced and realistic suggestions, if that's what you would like.

Weatherall, R. (2019). Writing the doctoral thesis differently. *Management Learning*, 50(1), 100–113.

This is a paper which advocates for the unleashing of a marvellous multiplicity of ways in which the act of writing the doctoral thesis could challenge the norms of research. I love its challenges and its possibilities. I hope it becomes part of a tsunami of new work that washes away all the things we think we know about how to do academic writing 'properly'.

HOW TO WRITE A JOURNAL ARTICLE

I have picked just two things out of this literature (which can tend towards the paternalistic and prescriptive in tone) because some folks like to see the picture on the box before they start the jigsaw. If you don't like these, check out their references and read around until you find something that suits you better. But remember that whilst all of them hold wisdom, none of them are 'true'. For example, as these hail from very different traditions of academic research, a quick read of both will show you that they do not meet each other's criteria!

Ecarnot, F., Seronde, M. F., Chopard, R., Schiele, F., & Meneveau, N. (2015). Writing a scientific article: A step-by-step guide for beginners. *European Geriatric Medicine*, 6(6), 573–579.

Fischer, E., Gopaldas, A., & Scaraboto, D. (2017). Why papers are rejected and how to get yours accepted: Advice on the construction of interpretive consumer research articles. *Qualitative Market Research*, 20(1), 60–67.

For a straightforward approach to the literature review, see Cronin, Ryan and Coughlan (2008) for some good advice.

PAPERS TO HELP YOU WORK OUT WHAT YOUR CONTRIBUTION SHOULD OR COULD BE

Locke, K., & Golden-Biddle, K. (1997). Constructing opportunities for contribution: Structuring intertextual coherence and 'problematizing' in organizational studies. *Academy of Management Journal*, 40(5), 1023–1062.

Whetten, D. A. (1989). What constitutes a theoretical contribution? *Academy of Management Review*, 14(4), 490–495.

RESPONDING TO REVIEWERS

Balan, S. (2022). Responding to reviewers' comments: Tips on handling challenging comments. *ChemTexts*, 8(3), 16.

This paper provides a clear and detailed description of the peer-review process, which I think will be really useful for folks new to this crazy game. The best thing about this paper, though, is the worked examples of how to address reviewers' comments. Getting negative or, worse, conflicting reviews can be really disheartening and I know a few folks who have given up on their papers or even their academic writing when they got one. Please don't do that! Stamp your feet a bit, have a bit of a sulk (one of my writing mentors recommends around five working days of sulking), take a deep breath and then work out which of Balan's eight categories best match the specific reviewer soup you find yourself knee-deep in and follow the advice given here. I cannot overstress the importance of writing a detailed letter to the reviewers that goes through their comments point by point: it can hugely increase the likelihood (and speed) of getting your paper accepted. Check out their reference list for other papers on this subject.

There is a whole special issue of the *Academy of Management* (one of the top journals in the management field) on the process of revising papers with reviewers' comments (2006, 49(2), 189–214). The interesting thing about this group of articles is that they deal with the journeys of two specific articles through the review process and that the same process is presented from the point of view of both the writer and the editor. The section on navigating the review process in Clark, Wright and Ketchen (2016) is very useful. See also Altman and Baruch (2008) for a survey of what academic authors in the management field do with their invitations to revise and resubmit, and an interesting categorisation of their reasons behind their choices; and Falkenberg and Soranno (2018) on what makes a good review.

BOOKS ABOUT WRITING

There are thousands of books about writing books. These fall into two main camps: books that want to tell you the story of how the author writes their books (writing memoirs); and books that want to tell you how to write your book (writing instructions). Some have a mixture of both (King, 2000). Good advice is to be found in all of these. If you can find one written by an author you love, they can be really inspiring.

In the writing memoirs, I have found a great deal of resonance with the writing processes I have elicited from academic writers for the purposes of this book. I found that Stephen King gets stuck! His book about writing (King, 2000), for example, sat in a drawer for more than 20 years! I love that he leaves a draft to go 'cold' for at least six weeks once it is complete before he tries to edit it. On the other hand, his deep distrust of the passive voice makes me slightly self-conscious about how much he would hate just about anything I have ever published! I read that Maya Angelou went to write in a tiny hotel room near her home every day that she used as an office (Tate, 2023). Structured days and ordered working habits are not what you might expect from such a mighty poet, but it seems that this sort of rigidity makes space for creativity rather than drowning it out. Over the years, I have sometimes read these out of interest in the writer's own story of their writing, both biographical and autobiographical, especially when I have run out of their fiction to read (Atwood, 2002; Barker, 1994, Walker, 1983).

A subset of this genre is books that focus on writing about the writing habits of others. One of the best is Claudia Tate's (2023) fabulous *Black Women Writers at Work*, presented as a curated set of interviews with some truly legendary writers. Long out of print, it was reprinted in 2023, 40 years after its first publication, and it is both a fascinating read and a rare insight into what a skilled interviewer looks like at work.

Sarah Stodola (2015) did a load of research on famous writers, living and dead. Her book shares lots of excellent factlets. My favourites were: Toni Morrison writes her first draft in pencil; Salman Rushdie starts writing before he is even dressed; Junot Díaz finds writing really difficult and also finds himself reading to avoid writing; Zadie Smith starts every writing session by reading her drafts from the beginning and editing as she goes. Can you imagine how long that took for a draft the size of White Teeth? Stodola concludes that there is no one definitive process: like Sword (2017), for every habit she uncovered amongst the great writers, she found another writer with the opposite habit.

In the writing instructions, I found all kinds of voices. Like a great proportion of books in the self-help vein, many of them advocate a single approach (see for example, Akinyemi, 2018 and Cameron, 1995 for examples of these sorts of systems). I have to mention Paul Silvia's *How to Write a Lot* (2018) and Robert Boice's *Professors as Writers* (1990) here, even though they belong in the 'books about academic writing' category, because they are both centred on a specific approach. Silvia (2018) advocates scheduling your writing time and then writing daily. Boice (1990) has a four-step plan to recovery. See what Helen Sword has to say about his work, or in fact any systems that start from the assumption that there is or could be a universal cure for notwriting (Sword, 2016). The thing with these is that you have to find one that will work for you personally, and that can take a bit of trial and error. Whatever kind of approach to motivation and words of wisdom you need, you will certainly find something amongst this vast library of advice: keep looking until you find a match. Here are some of my personal favourites.

Gilbert, E. (2016). *Big Magic: Creative Living beyond Fear*. Penguin.

This is my all time favourite book about writing. Elizabeth Gilbert (of *Eat, Pray, Love* fame) writes about her writing practice. She has a TED talk[6] which covers some of the same ground but I really would recommend the book as a way of cheering yourself up. It is lyrical and funny and honest. It is about the mysteries of the creative process but also about the routine of showing up day after day and the necessity of separating the creative work from the need to make a living.

Pressfield, S. (2002). *The War of Art: Break through the Blocks and Win Your Inner Creative Battles*. Black Irish Entertainment.

The war in question is between doing your creative work and the resistance to doing that creative work. The emphasis here is on reframing but it does offer two fundamental truths: (a) show up every day and do your creative work whether or not you feel like it and (b) resistance to your creativity will show up every day whether you do your work or not, whether you had a brilliant day yesterday or a bad month. See rule (a). A whole third of the book is dedicated to a multi-layered treatise on resistance. Which is genius. It is worth a read if you need a smile of recognition today.

Evans, B. & Smith, C. (2023). *Written: How to Keep Writing and Build a Habit That Lasts*. Icon Books.

This book starts from the point of view that one size fits nobody at all, which I love. It is one of the few books on writing that not only acknowledges that what works for one person may well not work for another, but also that what works for you *now* may not *always* work. Their central advice is to notice what works and does not work in supporting your own writing productivity and find your own writing 'rules'. They have conducted their own research on writers and also present a great overview of both the academic research on writing practices (academic and otherwise) and of what writers write about their writing. They have worked with all kinds of writers and many of the examples they give centre on academics so there is lots of relevance here, even if you prefer to read about academic writing. They run a writing coaching business called Prolifiko, which is discussed in the section on writing support below.

Cameron, J. (1995). *The Artist's Way: A Course in Discovering and Recovering Your Creative Self*. Pan Books.

This is a 12 week course in writing your way back to yourself and your creative purpose. I was given this book by a dear friend the very first time I was stuck. I moved house with it five times before I actually started to read it, more than 20 years later. In the intervening years I stopped believing that academic writing was 'different' to other kinds of writing and not *really* creative. When I did try to tackle it, I faded out after a few weeks. I started again a year later with renewed focus, determination and a group of other folk to be accountable with. We vowed to leave no one behind and so it actually turned into a [mumbles] month journey but we all got there in the end. Not to be undertaken lightly but also not to be dismissed. There are groups all over the world working through this together and I would advise getting yourself a crew to travel beside. Just do a search online for one in your time zone if not in your locale. The tools it offers are simple and robust and will bring you new practices as well as new insights. Can't say fairer than that. Definitely don't put it off for 20 years!

Lamott, A. (1995). *Bird by Bird: Some Instructions on Writing and Life*. Anchor.

This is a glorious read. There is some very sound writing advice, too (at any given moment you should only concern yourself with writing what you can fit in a one-inch picture frame; write 'short assignments' when you are stuck;

tackle large assignments bird by bird). Her many descriptions of what your mind does when you are mid-stuck are, for me, unparalleled. She also coined the term, 'shitty first draft'. The chapter on writing groups makes me sincerely glad that academics do not tend to have to read their work aloud to others, but reminds me how very much we need to have one or two readers that we implicitly trust to read what we think is our final draft. Quirky, funny and real.

RESOURCES FOR ACADEMIC MANAGERS AND RESEARCH DIRECTORS

Some of the issues discussed in this book are problems of the individual and can be solved by trying new things and looking at stuff in new ways. Some of them, though, are problems that are caused by the organisation and are being played out in the lives of the individuals. Other issues actually belong to the sector (Billig, 2013) and the organisation has to do its best to operate within these norms and still make academic life tenable for its people. I mention leadership here because this is the force that mediates between the organisation and the individual at the department or faculty level and between the sector norms and the organisation at the broader level. Good leadership at both very senior and middle-level university management has the ability to make a difference to the lives and the writing of individual academics. Never underestimate this. If you are in academic management (from leading the smallest team to the largest university), then start here.

What's Wrong with the Academy?

The fundamental purpose of academic writing has shifted over the last two generations. What began as a way to communicate with other scholars, disseminate thinking and results so as to 'join up' the academy and sync the brains of its members has become a way to demonstrate 'individual and institutional performance' (management speak intended) (McGrail et al., 2006). These papers might be useful if you are trying to take a step back and wonder how you got stuck in a particular type of institutional stuck (and what you might do to help your people deal with that). They might also make useful sources of evidence for people trying to convince academic managers to take a different tack. They might be the sort of thig you read if you wish to 'rock the boat, and … want to stay in it' Meyerson (2001, p. xi).

Alvesson, M., & Sandberg, J. (2014). Habitat and habitus: Boxed-in versus box-breaking research. *Organization Studies*, 35(7), 967–987.

Berg, M., & Seeber, B. K. (2016). *The Slow Professor: Challenging the Culture of Speed in the Academy*. University of Toronto Press.

This is a lovely celebration of slow research and also supplies a vast array of references to studies which show how and why speed is not helping scholarship.

Bozalek, V. (2017). Slow scholarship in writing retreats: A diffractive methodology for response-able pedagogies. *South African Journal of Higher Education*, 31(2), 40–57.
Miller Dyce, C., Ford, J. R., & Propst, B. S. (2022). Detoxing the trauma of academic writing for Black scholars: Vulnerability, authenticity, and healing. *Multicultural Perspectives*, 24(3), 170–179.

See also the special issue introduction for a useful overview of both the experiences and what is needed to address them:

Gist, C. D. (2022). Lessons on academic writing: What I learned about myself, us, and the work ahead. *Multicultural Perspectives*, 24(3), 180–183.

Grey, C., & Sinclair, A. (2006). Writing differently. *Organization*, 13(3), 443–453.
Heron, M., Gravett, K., & Yakovchuk, N. (2021). Publishing and flourishing: Writing for desire in higher education. *Higher Education Research & Development*, 40(3), 538–551.
Kiriakos, C. M., & Tienari, J. (2018). Academic writing as love. *Management Learning*, 49(3), 263–277.
Vachhani, S. J. (2019). Rethinking the politics of writing differently through écriture féminine. *Management Learning*, 50(1), 11–23.

For a great list of perceived barriers to academic writing from the point of view of the individual academic see Aydin, Yürük, Reisoğlu, and Goktas (2023). Using this work to start a discussion of the most pertinent issues for an individual, team or department could also help identify specific training, support and management solutions beyond the more general ones mentioned here. See also the first two chapters of Billig (2013) for a thorough and well-written overview of what is wrong with the academy and how exactly we got here.

Brown, B. (2018). *Dare to Lead: Brave Work. Tough Conversations. Whole Hearts.* Random House.

I make mention of a number of Brené Brown's ideas in this text (full disclosure: I am a Certified Dare to Lead Facilitator) and I wholeheartedly recommend *Dare to Lead*. This work can lay the foundations for much braver, more honest and open conversations about everything from values to performance. There is loads of material that supports the discussion and implementation of these leadership practices at the Dare to Lead Hub.[7]

Ajjawi, R., Crampton, P. E., & Rees, C. E. (2018). What really matters for successful research environments? A realist synthesis. *Medical Education*, 52(9), 936–950.

This is a lovely paper that hails from medicine and makes excellent use of the realist approach to tease out some interesting findings from a meta analysis of studies of academic research from the fields of medicine, medical education and education. The authors found that the same interventions played out differently in different contexts. One of the strengths of their analysis is that they consider not only some of the underlying mechanisms at play (time, researcher identity, researcher relationships), but also how these affect each other. It's a complex and insightful picture which I think has a lot to offer research management thinking.

McGrail, M. R., Rickard, C. M., & Jones, R. (2006). Publish or perish: A systematic review of interventions to increase academic publication rates. *Higher Education Research & Development*, 25(1), 19–35.

This study looks at how effective different types of intervention are in increasing academic publication rates. They examine studies on the outcomes of setting up writing support groups, delivering structured writing courses and using writing coaches. The writing group comes out as both the most widely used kind of intervention and also the most effective tool for increasing academic writing. The paper rounds up a range of studies into individual interventions and if you are looking to see what other departments have tried it makes a useful reference source.

There is an interesting tension between papers like this, which focus on the production of outputs as the proxy for success, and work like Heron et al. (2021), which look instead at the experience of the writing process. In trying to work out what actually works, be mindful that even if you intend to simply 'count' outputs that you need to take a long-term view: Šimić and his colleagues (2021) found that the effects of attending an 18 hour programme of writing workshops took three years to peak!

Stanier, M. B. (2010). *Do More Great Work*. Workman Publishing.

This book is a series of 15 maps for you to complete to help you figure out how you spend your limited time and attention and give you tools to reconsider that unconscious distribution. It is particularly helpful for folks who unthinkingly prioritise the urgent over the important, and are therefore 'too busy to write'. It can help you think about the difference between work you are good at and work you love. This was a revelation for me. I exhausted myself with decades of doing work I was good at and, by the time I got to the questions in this book, I had no idea what work I loved. It took me a lot of soul searching and wild experiments to find the end of my great work thread and this book definitely played a part in that process. It would also be a good framework for scholars wondering 'what sort of academic do I want to be?'. There are lots of different ways to be successful in this arena and success will come faster if you choose just one, and with less cost if you choose one that is suited to your innate strengths and interests. Work through it yourself, with colleagues or with the people in your team. Are there ways you could arrange your departmental workload (all of it, not just the visible, legitimate work) so that everyone can do some of their great work inside their day job?

ACCOUNTABILITY

Bestseller Experiment

If you'd like to see just how small an amount of accountability you need to make a difference to your writing progress, then look up the Bestseller Experiment.[8] This is an online community run by Mark Desvaux and Mark Stay. It began with a podcast with them interviewing writers whilst they took on a challenge to write a bestseller in a year. Which they did! You can sign up and promise to write 200 words every day along with thousands of others with a team goal to write a billion words. Every day you write your words, count them, log in and post your progress. It could not be more simple and for some crazy reason it does actually work. I have used this when I have been really stuck and the effect of just reporting your word count daily to a website never fails to surprise me. It cheers me up and cheers me on. They also have a Bestseller Academy you can pay to join where they pass on all their amassed wisdom from their experiments. Check out the podcast and blog to access loads, and I mean LOADS, of advice from authors and interesting content for free.

Academic Ladder and Prolifiko (see Writing coaching next) also offer accountability systems.

WRITING COACHING

Prolifiko

This is a UK-based service for all kinds of writers focused on writing practice. I found them through their free Sprint events where they help you track your writing progress over seven days, setting and reporting on micro goals for each day. This is a great way to get some momentum going on a daily habit in the company of others. I have done this a few times when I have completely ground to a halt and found it a really kind, positive and supportive community. They also hold events and offer coaching programmes which are professional and enthusiastic in equal measure. Their book, *Written* (Bec Evans & Chris Smith, 2023), is a great resource if you are curious to know more about what has been written about writing (see Books about writing in this section). See also their study of academic writing.[9]

Academic Ladder

Academic Ladder[10] is an online service focused on increasing productivity in academic writing. It is quite heavily biased towards the United States (US) tenure system in terms of references and advice, but the advice is pretty sound and generalisable. They work with academics at all career stages from dissertation (a shorter version of a doctoral thesis, but at the same level [see Glossary entry on Thesis] to tenure [or what they call a 'full professor', which is the US equivalent of a professorship/chair – they use the term professor to address any teaching staff with or without a chair]). They have lots of blogs and articles to browse but they offer two main things: a writing club and coaching. The writing club is where you subscribe to an online accountability system for small groups of academics who log in to state their tasks and log their progress and congratulate each other. A coach will give you a prod if you get too silent. I have used this when what I needed was a little structure and a little polite and cheerful surveillance and it has been known to get me unstuck. They also offer group and one-to-one coaching.

CO-WORKING COMMUNITIES

I love co-working and these take the hassle and compromise out of coordinating times with people you know. Just sprinkling this tiny bit of accountability on my day is productive and weirdly life affirming for me.

Caveday

Caveday[11] is an online organisation dedicated to co-working. You pay a subscription and then you can schedule co-working sessions (caves) where you show up for an hour or three and work. Each cave has a guide who will get everyone to say what they are going to work on at the start of each session and congratulate you on whatever you have achieved at the end. They will make you stretch, take short breaks and tell other humans your hourly goals in two minute breakout rooms. This works for me like magic. They are really friendly and efficient. There are loads of caves every day and you can do solo caves if none of the group sessions suit. People are in caves to create focus for every imaginable kind of task. I save it for my most boring work tasks and I have ground through many a spreadsheet whilst someone else finalises their quilting patterns, does daily yoga or writes novels or PhDs. Sign up for a free trial to see if they are for you.

Shut Up & Write

For those of you who like to be amongst creatives, I recommend Shut Up & Write.[12] I love to work alongside poets, novelists and script writers, and I am seldom the only academic in the group. They have a large number of online events you can join for free each day. I've never been to a face-to-face event, but it looks like there are events held in a lot of major cities. The slots vary from an hour to three hours in duration. A host will invite everyone to share their task for the day with the group at the start and a shared timer lets you know when to come and share your progress again at the end. Lots of the time slots are regular, repeating each day or week at the same time, which is helpful if you want to build a regular writing habit. They are a really welcoming bunch.

Writer's Hour

Writer's Hour[13] is a free initiative, run by the London Writer's Salon. It comprises four one hour online writing sprints each weekday, all held at 8am in different time zones. It is always time to get an hour of writing in before work somewhere in the world! Sign up for whichever one(s) you prefer. It's a big, supportive and good-humoured group with over 100 people on a video call and it is managed by a pair of facilitators. They welcome new members, ask everyone to write in the chat what they will work on and then share an inspirational quote about writing and raise a glass to start your session. At the end of the session, you will go back to the chat to report on progress, the facilitators will each speak to someone about what they are working on and then close the session with a one word check in the chat. The main difference between this community and the others I have mentioned is that when you sign up, you sign up for that hour every weekday, which promotes writing at the same time every day which could really help habit building, but it is just a wee bit too organised for the likes of me! The other communities also have regular slots, but you can choose to sign up for one or all of them.

HABITS

Stanier, M. B. (2016). *6½ Habit Gurus*. Box of Crayons.

If you want to know more about the science of habits start here. This is a free e-book about how to change habits which can be downloaded as part of the free resources for his book *The Coaching Habit* (Stanier, 2016).[14] It runs through a synopsis of six great writers who all have something to say about how to form habits and picks out their best piece of advice (great for folks short on time or on motivation to read whole books but also short on excuses for those of us who like to use reading as a way to put off starting). If your challenge with the business of writing a small amount every day is the 'every day' part, then these folks have lots to offer. The last section considers habit apps which help build accountability and finish lines for you to celebrate crossing.

Clear, J. (2018). *Atomic Habits: An Easy and Proven Way to Build Good Habits and Break Bad Ones*. Penguin.

This book aims to give you a better insight into how habits are formed. It is well written and persuasive and it might appeal to you if you are trying to change your writing habits. It takes the view that habits compound over time but not in a linear fashion (just in case you were wondering why it feels like your progress isn't multiplying, even though you are adding in some writing every day). He is also pretty dismissive of goals and instead values the systems we put in place as the real agents of change. He offers a four-step process for building new habits and offers four laws of behaviour change to go with them: make it obvious; make it attractive; make it easy; and make it satisfying. It is easy to understand how you could apply these to your writing habits in everything from reducing your resistance to getting started to understanding your own self-sabotage routines. The book is practical and packed full of stories and metaphors to illustrate his points.

ONLINE RESOURCES

There are lots of places online where people talk about academic writing. Some of my favourites are the following.

Professor Pat Thomson writing as **Patter**. She is a professor of education in the UK and her clear and straightforward explanations are aimed at decoding academia for us all. You can find her on Facebook at 'writingwithpatter' and her website.[15]

I would also recommend the **Thesis Whisperer**, written by Professor Inger Mewburn in Australia. She has built up a huge database of content on everything and anything you can think of, all written in a conversational style that will make you smile.[16]

The **Thesis Doctor** in South Africa is essentially a proofreading and editing service, but their Facebook page[17] has gathered together a load of papers and diagrams from other sources, making it a useful place to browse if you are stuck with something specific.

APPS THAT STOP THE INTERNET

If you find yourself struggling to ignore email, or the lure of social media (you're looking at a grown woman who allows herself less screen time on

Facebook than she allows her children because otherwise she can lose an hour of her life without noticing) or you find the routine of switching off every notification just too long and annoying, then you might be interested to know that you can get apps which 'silence' any programs you select on your computer for a specified amount of time. I haven't tried any of these, but I do know folks who swear by them.

Freedom[18] is a subscription app that works on all operating systems and browsers. It allows you to set a schedule of work hours when it will switch off specific programs, sites or apps. So, whether your personal temptation is interior décor on Instagram, online shopping or cat videos on Facebook, you can make sure that there are times of the day when you just can't access them. You can sign up for a free trial to see whether it suits your work habits before you buy it.

SelfControl[19] is an open-code, free app that does the same thing for Mac users. You can set it to block anything on the internet for a specified amount of time. The logo isn't a skull for no reason, though: once you have set the timer going there is no way around it until your time is up, even if you delete the application in desperation!

3 steps to getting
unstuck

1. be well
2. try new things
seek out support
shift your thinking
3. practise 1 & 2

NOTES

1.   https://writersdiet.com/base/base/.
2.   www.ucl.ac.uk/ioe/events/2023/jan/academic-writing-and-neurodiversity-pedagogies-inclusion.
3.   https://phdisabled.wordpress.com/.
4.   https://scholarstudioblog.wordpress.com/2015/11/15/part-3-tools-and-resources-for-neurodiverse-graduate-students/.
5.   https://adhdcollective.com/adhd-and-college-writing-papers/.
6.   www.ted.com/talks/elizabeth_gilbert_your_elusive_creative_genius?utm_campaign=tedspread&utm_medium=referral&utm_source=tedcomshare.
7.   https://brenebrown.com/hubs/dare-to-lead/.
8.   https://bestsellerexperiment.com/.
9.   https://prolifiko.com/wp-content/uploads/2019/03/Life-of-a-Productive-Scholar_-Key-Findings-Report.pdf.
10.   www.academicladder.com.
11.   www.caveday.org.
12.   www.shutupwrite.com.
13.   www.writershour.com.
14.   Go to https://www.mbs.works/coaching-habit-book/#resources and sign up to get a free copy of this pdf.
15.   https://patthomson.net/.
16.   https://thesiswhisperer.com/.
17.   www.facebook.com/thethesisdoctor/.
18.   www.freedom.to.
19.   https://selfcontrolapp.com/.

Where do I start? Flowcharts

There are a lot of suggestions of things you could do in this book, and a lot of places you could start.

So, if:

- you'd like a wee bit of help with finding a place to start;
- you want to find a place that speaks to your specific kind of stuck;
- you find it hard to decide;
- you are a visual thinker; or
- you are in too much of a hurry to read this whole thing right now, thank you,

then you will find some flowcharts in this section that might orient you in this advice-fest.

There are six flowcharts, each centred on a slightly different set of challenges. If you're not sure which one to choose, read a few and see what resonates most. In each one you will find both general advice (in grey) and signposts to specific sections from this book.

OK, LET'S DO IT!

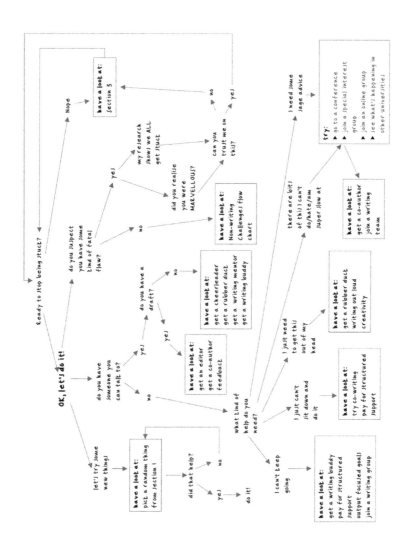

WRITING SKILLS CHALLENGES

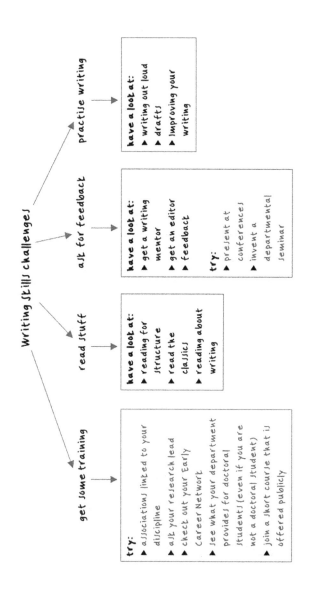

Writing skills challenges

practise writing

have a look at:
- writing out loud
- drafts
- Improving your writing

ask for feedback

have a look at:
- get a writing mentor
- get an editor
- feedback

try:
- present at conferences
- invent a departmental seminar

read stuff

have a look at:
- reading for structure
- read the classics
- reading about writing

get some training

try:
- associations linked to your discipline
- ask your research lead
- check out your Early Career Network
- see what your department provides for doctoral students (even if you are not a doctoral student)
- join a short course that is offered publicly

TIME CHALLENGES

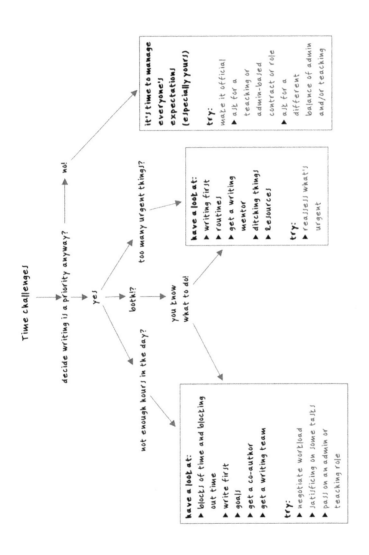

NON-WRITING CHALLENGES

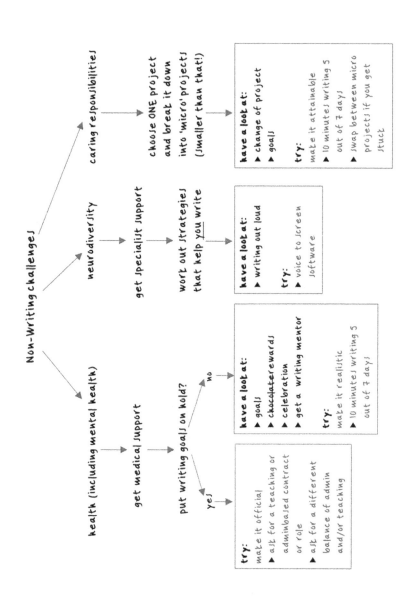

Non-Writing challenges

health (including mental health)
- get medical support
- put writing goals on hold?

  yes
  try:
  make it official
  - ask for a teaching or admin-based contract or role
  - ask for a different balance of admin and/or teaching

  no
  have a look at:
  - goals
  - chocolate rewards
  - celebration
  - get a writing mentor

  try:
  make it realistic
  - 10 minutes writing 5 out of 7 days

neurodiversity
- get specialist support
- work out strategies that help _you_ write

  have a look at:
  - writing out loud

  try:
  - voice to screen software

caring responsibilities
- choose ONE project and break it down into 'micro' projects (smaller than that!)

  have a look at:
  - change of project
  - goals

  try:
  make it attainable
  - 10 minutes writing 5 out of 7 days
  - swap between micro projects if you get stuck

PSYCHOLOGICAL CHALLENGES

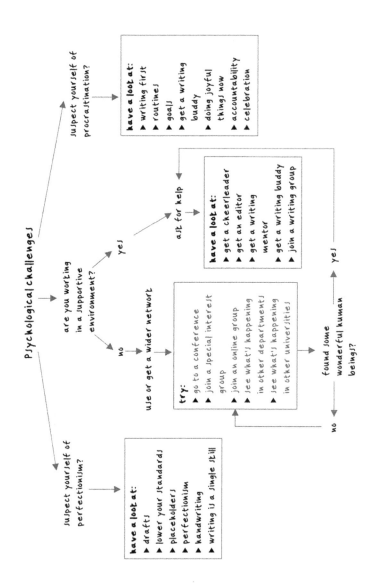

CHALLENGES WITH A SPECIFIC WRITING PROJECT

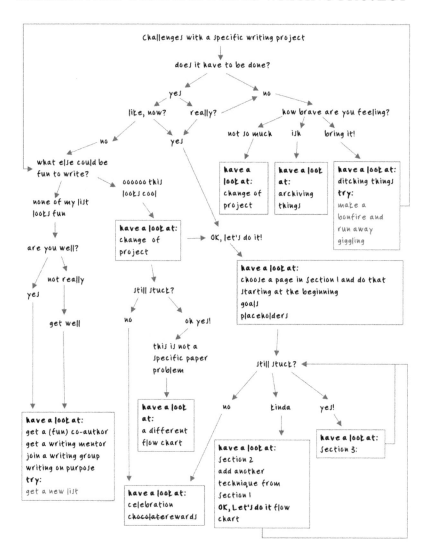

Glossary of UK terms

The majority of my experience of academia and academic writing has played out within a UK context. Although loads of things about what it is like to be an academic (and all of the things about getting stuck with your academic writing) are pretty similar in other contexts, what we call things isn't. Here is a list of terms which I use in this book in a UK-specific way. Many don't have exact definitions, and the explanations I have offered here won't seem quite right to all my UK colleagues, because I have gone for 'typical' accounts rather than those which will cover every eventuality. I have tried to describe them here in a more general way in the hope that it will make what I have written more accessible for as many folks as possible.

Border Agency: Now officially retitled UK Visas and Immigration, the Border Agency is the folks who turn up to check people's visas. At the time of writing, students with study visas had to attend a certain number of classes in order to be allowed to be classed as 'studying full time' and universities therefore had to keep immaculate records of their attendance so that the Border Agency could audit them at any moment to ensure that people were complying with the terms of their visa. The individual consequences of not complying are not good.

Journal lists: In the UK there are lists of journals that have been drawn up to guide folks as to how their paper might be scored in the Research Excellence Framework (REF) review, according to the journal it is published in. Have a look at the Chartered Association of Business Schools Academic Journal Guide[1] for a UK example. The REF panel does not rank journals; it states that it reads every output that is submitted to it and judges its merit independently of where it is published, so these lists are not official and some people are quite cross about them (Hussain, 2015; Mingers and Willmott, 2013), but they persist regardless. The UK isn't the only country to have these lists: Australia has one for business journals (ABDC Journal Quality List, Australian Business Deans Council[2]) and I know some US universities have 'tenure-approved' lists for some disciplines.

Research Excellence Framework (REF): The REF (previously Research Assessment Exercise) is an evaluation of all UK universities carried out approximately every five years by panels of experts. The published outputs of every researcher are assessed and scored from unclassified (yikes) to 4* (yay) by peers from their own discipline. The scores are added up to give a subject score for every discipline for every university. Scores are also given for the research environment and the impact. These scores determine the amount of government research funding each university will get. There are similarly charming systems in other countries: Australia had the Research Quality Framework, which is now Excellence in Research for Australia, New Zealand has its Performance-Based Research Fund and Italy has Valutazione della Qualità della Ricerca, for example. Although academic journals are not scored by the REF panels, unofficial ranking lists exist in many disciplines (see entry for Journal lists for some examples) that associate the REF classifications with academic journals. Thus, you might hear an academic being referred to as being '4x4', implying that she has published 4 articles in so-called 4* journals during the current REF period. It also lends itself to people creating subject and then university ranking tables[3] based on their amalgamated REF scores. Then the game playing begins ...

Science and Engineering Research Council: The Science and Engineering Research Council was one of several discipline-specific research councils that funded doctoral students, research fellows and research grants for UK academics by distributing public research funds through competitions. It was split up into three smaller Research Councils in 1994. All the UK Research Councils have now been gathered together as UK Research and Innovation.

Thesis: In the UK, many doctorates are still done by 'tome', i.e. by spending four years full time doing independent research and writing a book. Candidates write around 80,000 words (around 350 pages), depending on the subject, which is called their thesis. In the US, doctoral study takes candidates five or six years and includes advanced classes in their subject that candidates need to pass before they can write a book, which is 100–200 pages long and is called their dissertation. In the UK the term 'dissertation' is much more likely to be used for undergraduate and masters degree final research papers. US friends: when I say 'thesis', please hear 'dissertation'.

Typos: This term is a shortening of 'typographical errors', which literally means typing (or typesetting) incorrect characters but has been extended in academic parlance to mean all the lovely errors of grammar and syntax that we regularly commits.

NOTES

1. https://charteredabs.org/academic-journal-guide-2021/.
2. https://abdc.edu.au/abdc-journal-quality-list/.
3. www.timeshighereducation.com/sites/default/files/Attachments/2014/12/17/k/a/s/over-14-01.pdf.

Methods

There are three strands of data that have been gathered in order to write this book.

The first is autoethnographic. It centres on writing, speaking and teaching I have done about my (lack of) writing over the years. The first layer of analysis was done in service of talking to others about being stuck with writing. These data have been presented in two main ways: through presentation and as part of one-to-one writing support:

- Presentation: These ideas about writing have been presented in a number of seminars given to doctoral students (Strathclyde, 1995; Leeds/York/Sheffield, 2016) and post-doctoral peers (Lancaster, 1996) and later colleagues (Sheffield, 2005; Robert Gordon University, 2019) and/or mixed groups (Strathclyde, 2018) over the course of my career. The material on synthesis and critique has its origins in the many 100s of happy hours I've spent teaching academic writing as part of research methods courses over the years to undergraduate, masters and doctoral students.
- One-to-one writing support: these ideas have been developed for and by wonderful conversations with students and colleagues writing doctoral theses. Many of the distinctions presented here were surfaced and cultivated in order to support and inspire the doctoral students I was supervising (1998–2019) or managing (2009–2016).

The more I discussed my writing habits and cycles with others, the more I began to see them as much less odd and problematic than I had imagined. What started out as a way to understand and shift my own practices became a mission to break the taboos around being open about the struggles of academic writing and help others get unstuck. The second strand of data crosses over between my concentration on myself as a writer and my interest in the writing practices of others, and my gradual realisation that 'stuck' is a more or less universal experience for academic writers.

During these first two phases of data collection, the sampling was open, ideas were widely discussed and feedback was kept as contemporaneous notes, which were used to refine presentations and teaching materials but also to form the foundation layer of data for this book.

Finally, once my attention turned to writing a book that would set out my ideas more formally and comprehensively, I undertook a set of semistructured interviews with academic writers in order to refine my theory of stuck and test the viability of my assumptions more formally. During 2018 I developed a relational sampling strategy. I started by speaking with people from all levels of their academic careers who either struggled to write or who were prolific writers. I reached theoretical saturation quite quickly, and then focused my final, discriminate sample on the academic writing of scientists. This final data collection phase centred on the applicability of my findings for science colleagues and thus the final tranche of semistructured interviews was done with folks writing in some of the science literatures.

The semistructured interviews were transcribed and the transcripts were analysed using an iterative, constant comparison approach. Themes were developed from these data and stories were selected for inclusion on the basis that they added either nuance or difference to my own collected stories. All of the headings in the book were developed from these two data sets (notes and transcripts) and the diagrams surfaced from the semistructured interview data. The flowcharts come from an accumulation of writing support delivered one to one where 'patterns' or archetypes of stuck started to become apparent over many years.

About the author

Seonaidh (pronounced 'Shona' in case you were wondering) has been involved in academic writing since she started her PhD at the University of Stirling in 1991. This is where she first developed her skills in writing, notwriting and, eventually, NOTwriting. Following a post-doc position as a research assistant at Strathclyde University, where she learned notwritingatall, she was a research fellow at Lancaster University, where she finally began to understand academic writing and also found the joy of writing with others for the first time. These last two were not unrelated.

Seonaidh joined Sheffield University Management School in 1998, where she taught business strategy and research methods. She was very happy there because the people were marvellous, but they made the mistake of letting her go on sabbatical to Orkney and she realised you couldn't see the sea from Sheffield. At all.

In 2003 Seonaidh joined Aberdeen Business School at the Robert Gordon University as part of a university-wide research development programme. She stayed there a very long time, talked to a huge number of people about their research and was awarded a Chair in 2013. Because she did eventually write a load of things, and some of them were quite good.

Over the years, Seonaidh has had the great honour of supporting many doctoral students, including around 20 of her own. This is how she learned that notwriting, NOTwriting and notwritingatall were not things she alone excelled at but are in fact almost ubiquitous. It is also how she first uncovered the joyfulness of helping folks do the things she found so hard to do herself.

Seonaidh worked for Innovate UK for a few years, although she has never actually been to Swindon. Now she is working at UHI Orkney where she can see the sea from her office window. From 2024 to 2026 Seonaidh will also be Visiting Professor at the Hunter Centre at the University of Strathclyde in Glasgow, talking about the joys (and 'joys') of academic writing with anyone who will listen.

References

Academy of Management Journal (2006). Special issue. 49(2), 189–214. Authors: Agarwal, Echambadi, Franco & Sarkar (191–196); Bergh (197–202); Rynes (189–190, 208–214); Siebert (203–207).

Adams, D. (1979). *The Hitchhiker's Guide to the Galaxy*. Pan Books.

Ajjawi, R., Crampton, P. E., & Rees, C. E. (2018). What really matters for successful research environments? A realist synthesis. *Medical Education*, 52(9), 936–950.

Akinyemi, N. S. (2018). *Write the Book, Sis! An Interactive Guide to Writing a Powerful Book Your Audience Will Want to Read*. YBF Publishing.

Altman, Y., & Baruch, Y. (2008). Strategies for revising and resubmitting papers to refereed journals. *British Journal of Management*, 19(1), 89–101.

Alvesson, M., & Sandberg, J. (2014). Habitat and habitus: Boxed-in versus box-breaking research. *Organization Studies*, 35(7), 967–987.

Atwood, M. (2002). *On Writers and Writing*. Virago.

Aydin, A., Yürük, S. E., Reisoğlu, İ., & Goktas, Y. (2023). Main barriers and possible enablers of academicians while publishing. *Scientometrics*, 128(1), 623–650.

Balan, S. (2022). Responding to reviewers' comments: Tips on handling challenging comments. *ChemTexts*, 8(3), 16.

Barker, J. (1994). *The Brontës*. Orion Publishing.

Berg, M., & Seeber, B. K. (2016). *The Slow Professor: Challenging the Culture of Speed in the Academy*. University of Toronto Press.

Billig, M. (2013). *Learn to Write Badly: How to Succeed in the Social Sciences*. Cambridge University Press.

Boice, R. (1990). *Professors as Writers: A Self-Help Guide to Productive Writing*. New Forums Press.

Bowers, J. M. (2019). *Tolkien's Lost Chaucer*. Oxford University Press.

Bozalek, V. (2017). Slow scholarship in writing retreats: A diffractive methodology for response-able pedagogies. *South African Journal of Higher Education*, 31(2), 40–57.

Brabazon, T. (2010). How to get students through their PhD thesis. *Times Higher Education*, 22 September.

Brennan, A., Chugh, J., & Kline, T. (2002). Traditional versus open office design: A longitudinal field study. *Environment and Behavior*, 34(3), 279–299.

Brown, B. (2015). *Daring Greatly: How the Courage to Be Vulnerable Transforms the Way We Live, Love, Parent, and Lead*. Penguin.

Brown, B. (2017). *Braving the Wilderness: The Quest for True Belonging and the Courage to Stand Alone*. Random House.

Brown, B. (2018). *Dare to Lead: Brave Work. Tough Conversations. Whole Hearts*. Random House.

Burn, S. M., & Oskamp, S. (1986). Increasing community recycling with persuasive communication and public commitment. *Journal of Applied Social Psychology*, 16(1), 29–41.

Cameron, J. (1995). *The Artist's Way: A Course in Discovering and Recovering Your Creative Self.* Pan Books.

Cirillo, F. (2018). *The Pomodoro Technique: The Life-Changing Time-Management System.* Virgin Books.

Clark, T., Wright, M., & Ketchen, Jr., D. J. (Eds) (2017). *How to Get Published in the Best Management Journals.* Edward Elgar Publishing.

Clear, J. (2018). *Atomic Habits: An Easy and Proven Way to Build Good Habits and Break Bad Ones.* Penguin.

Cronin, P., Ryan, F., & Coughlan, M. (2008). Undertaking a literature review: a step-by-step approach. *British Journal of Nursing,* 17(1), 38–43.

Danielsson, C. B., & Bodin, L. (2008). Office type in relation to health, well-being, and job satisfaction among employees. *Environment and Behavior,* 40(5), 636–668.

Ecarnot, F., Seronde, M. F., Chopard, R., Schiele, F., & Meneveau, N. (2015). Writing a scientific article: A step-by-step guide for beginners. *European Geriatric Medicine,* 6(6), 573–579.

Evans, B., & Smith, C. (2019). The life of a productive scholarly author: How academics write, the barriers they face and why publishers and institutions should feel optimistic. https://prolifiko.com/wp-content/uploads/2019/03/Life-of-a-Productive -Scholar_-Key-Findings-Report.pdf

Evans, B., & Smith, C. (2023). *Written: How to Keep Writing and Build a Habit That Lasts.* Icon Books.

Falkenberg, L. J., & Soranno, P. A. (2018). Reviewing reviews: An evaluation of peer reviews of journal article submissions. *Limnology and Oceanography Bulletin,* 27(1), 1–5.

Fischer, E., Gopaldas, A., & Scaraboto, D. (2017). Why papers are rejected and how to get yours accepted: Advice on the construction of interpretive consumer research articles. *Qualitative Market Research,* 20(1), 60–67.

Fontana-Giusti, G. (2013). *Foucault for Architects.* Routledge.

Foxwell, J., Alderson-Day, B., Fernyhough, C., & Woods, A. (2020). 'I've learned I need to treat my characters like people': Varieties of agency and interaction in writers' experiences of their characters' voices. *Consciousness and Cognition,* 79, 102901.

Gilbert, E. (2016). *Big Magic: Creative Living beyond Fear.* Penguin.

Gist, C. D. (2022). Lessons on academic writing: What I learned about myself, us, and the work ahead. *Multicultural Perspectives,* 24(3), 180–183.

Grey, C., & Sinclair, A. (2006). Writing differently. *Organization,* 13(3), 443–453.

Gunesekera, R., & Kennedy, A. L. (2015). *Novel Writing: A Writers' and Artists' Companion.* Bloomsbury.

Hemingway, E. (1964). *A Moveable Feast.* Johnathan Cape.

Henriksen, D. (2016). The rise in co-authorship in the social sciences (1980–2013). *Scientometrics,* 107(2), 455–476.

Heron, M., Gravett, K., & Yakovchuk, N. (2021). Publishing and flourishing: Writing for desire in higher education. *Higher Education Research & Development,* 40(3), 538–551.

Hussain, S. (2015). Journal list fetishism and the 'sign of 4' in the ABS guide: A question of trust? *Organization,* 22(1), 119–138.

Jensen, J. (2017). *Write No Matter What: Advice for Academics.* University of Chicago Press.

Kamler, B., & Thomson, P. (2008). The failure of dissertation advice books: Toward alternative pedagogies for doctoral writing. *Educational Researcher,* 37(8), 507–514.

Keyes, R. (2003). *The Writer's Book of Hope: Getting from Frustration to Publication*. Henry Holt & Company.

King, S. (2000). *On Writing: A Memoir of the Craft*. Simon and Schuster.

Kiriakos, C. M., & Tienari, J. (2018). Academic writing as love. *Management Learning*, 49(3), 263–277.

Lamott, A. (1995). *Bird by Bird: Some Instructions on Writing and Life*. Anchor.

Locke, K., & Golden-Biddle, K. (1997). Constructing opportunities for contribution: Structuring intertextual coherence and 'problematizing' in organizational studies. *Academy of Management Journal*, 40(5), 1023–1062.

McDonald, S. (2005). Studying actions in context: A qualitative shadowing method for organizational research. *Qualitative Research*, 5(4), 455–473.

McDonald, S., Gan, B. C., Fraser, S. S., Oke, A., & Anderson, A. R. (2015). A review of research methods in entrepreneurship 1985–2013. *International Journal of Entrepreneurial Behavior & Research*, 21(3), 291–315.

McGrail, M. R., Rickard, C. M., & Jones, R. (2006). Publish or perish: A systematic review of interventions to increase academic publication rates. *Higher Education Research & Development*, 25(1), 19–35.

Meyerson, D. E. (2001). *Tempered Radicals: How People Use Difference to Inspire Change at Work*. Harvard Business School Press.

Miller Dyce, C., Ford, J. R., & Propst, B. S. (2022). Detoxing the trauma of academic writing for Black scholars: Vulnerability, authenticity, and healing. *Multicultural Perspectives*, 24(3), 170–179.

Mingers, J., & Willmott, H. (2013). Taylorizing business school research: On the 'one best way' performative effects of journal ranking lists. *Human Relations*, 66(8), 1051–1073.

Oshima, A., & Hogue, A. (2007). *Introduction to Academic Writing*. Pearson/Longman.

Pang, A. S. K. (2016). *Rest: Why You Get More Done When You Work Less*. Basic Books.

Pratchett, T. (1993). *Small Gods*. Corgi Books.

Pressfield, S. (2002). *The War of Art: Break Through the Blocks and Win Your Inner Creative Battles*. Black Irish Entertainment.

Rath, T. (2007). *StrengthsFinder 2.0*. Simon and Schuster.

Silvia, P. J. (2018). *How to Write a Lot: A Practical Guide to Productive Academic Writing*. American Psychological Association.

Šimić, J., Marušić, M., Gelo, M., Šaravanja, N., Mišak, A., & Marušić, A. (2021). Long-term outcomes of 2-day training on planning and writing research on publication output of medical professionals: 11-year cohort study. *Learned Publishing*, 34(4), 666–674.

Sims, G. (2017). *Why Mummy Drinks*. HaperCollins Publishers.

Smith, R., McElwee, G., McDonald, S., & Dodd, S. D. (2013). Qualitative entrepreneurship authorship: Antecedents, processes and consequences. *International Journal of Entrepreneurial Behaviour and Research*, 19(4), 364–386.

Stanier, M. B. (2010). *Do More Great Work*. Workman Publishing.

Stanier, M. B. (2016). *The Coaching Habit: Say Less, Ask More & Change the Way You Lead Forever*. Page Two Books, Inc.

Stodola, S. (2015). *Process: The Writing Lives of Great Authors*. Amazon Publishing.

Sword, H. (2016). 'Write every day!': A mantra dismantled. *International Journal for Academic Development*, 21(4), 312–322.

Sword, H. (2017). *Air & Light & Time & Space: How Successful Academics Write*. Harvard University Press.

Tate, C. (Ed.) (2023). *Black Women Writers at Work*. Haymarket Books.

Taylor, M., Hodges, S. D., & Kohányi, A. (2003). The illusion of independent agency: Do adult fiction writers experience their characters as having minds of their own? *Imagination, Cognition and Personality*, 22(4), 361–380.

Tietze, A., Galam, S., & Hofmann, P. (2020). Crediting multi-authored papers to single authors. *Physica A: Statistical Mechanics and Its Applications*, 554, 124652.

Uwizeye, D., Karimi, F., Thiong'o, C., Syonguvi, J., Ochieng, V., Kiroro, F., … & Wao, H. (2021). Factors associated with research productivity in higher education institutions in Africa: A systematic review. *AAS Open Research*, 4.

Vachhani, S. J. (2019). Rethinking the politics of writing differently through écriture féminine. *Management Learning*, 50(1), 11–23.

Van Marrewijk, A., & Van den Ende, L. (2018). Changing academic work places: The introduction of open-plan offices in universities. *Journal of Organizational Change Management*, 31(5), 1119–1137.

Walker, A. (1983). *In Search of Our Mother's Garden*. Harcourt, Brace, and Jovanovich.

Wallbank, A. J. (2022). *Academic Writing and Dyslexia: A Visual Guide to Writing at University*. Taylor & Francis.

Weatherall, R. (2019). Writing the doctoral thesis differently. *Management Learning*, 50(1), 100–113.

Whetten, D. A. (1989). What constitutes a theoretical contribution? *Academy of Management Review*, 14(4), 490–495.

Wolcott, H. F. (2008). *Writing Up Qualitative Research*. Sage.

Woodfield, A. (2021). *This Is Your Moment: Find and Follow Your Unique Path in Life and Your Business*. Panoma Press.

Index